WHAT PEOPLE ARE

GODDESS C.

A strong, courageous book that will either set your teeth on edge or make you laugh with joy.
Jean Houston, Ph.D – World-renowned American scholar, lecturer, author, and philosopher active in the "human potential movement". Adviser to political leaders, UNICEF, and the United Nations Development Group training leaders in the new field of Social Artistry.

Karen Tate's inspirational work celebrates Goddess spirituality and encourages all women to rediscover their sacred history, to break the shackles that patriarchal culture has imposed on them, and to take action for the preservation of our Mother Earth. Her meditations on the state of our world, past, present and future, are profoundly engaging.
Barbara G. Walker – Beloved Foremother and author of *The Woman's Encyclopedia of Myths and Secrets, The Woman's Dictionary of Symbols and Sacred Objects, The Crone, Feminist Fairy Tales,* and *Man Made God.*

A magnificent work, carefully researched, inspiring language, beautifully organized. To anyone who can only read one good book about the Goddess, I would recommend this work. Karen Tate is in love with life, and with the ancient wisdom. A very generous author who is a sister soul in revolution.
Zsuzsanna Budapest – Pioneer in the Women's Spirituality Movement, women's rights activist, journalist, playwright, songwriter, teacher, evolutionary priestess, visionary and author of many books including *The Holy Book of Women's Mysteries.*

Drawing on her eclectic experiences as teacher, interviewer, scholar, traveler, and liturgist, Karen Tate has created in Goddess Calling a

powerful synthesis of well-chosen information, reflective observation and poetic prose. This unique volume combines astute analysis of present day social and political realities with soothing meditations, a welcomed addition to the conversation about the female divine. Throughout, goddesses from varied times and locations become accessible and embodied providing an impressive work of thealogy. Goddess Calling is an invaluable resource when crafting meaningful rituals as well as a helpful companion for individual study, inspiration and personal development.
Elizabeth Fisher – Author of *Rise Up and Call Her Name: A Woman-honoring Journey into Earth-based Spiritualities.*

Political Perspectives to challenge oppression, Ecofeminist Thealogy to empower action, Goddess Meditations to feed the Soul.
Rev. Selena Fox – Psychotherapist, environmentalist, Pagan rights activist, High Priestess of Circle Sanctuary, and author of *Goddess Communion* and *When Goddess is God.*

Goddess Calling is a valuable resource for those regularly called upon to create services or ceremonies for the exploration of Goddess Spirituality. Karen Tate offers a selection of "Messages" relating the values of Goddess Spirituality – as expressed through the sacred myths of ancient and living Goddess traditions – to today's society, politics, and culture. Then she provides a series of "Meditations" that can help participants awaken those Goddess values in their own lives. Karen brings her deep experience with Goddess Spirituality and the liveliness of her long-running internet radio program, Voices of the Sacred Feminine, to this inspirational book."
M. Isidora Forrest - Author of *Isis Magic: Cultivating a Relationship with the Goddess of 10,000 Names* and *Offering to Isis, Knowing the Goddess Through Her Sacred Symbols*

Women all over the world are rising up to create their own circles, churches and organizations to empower themselves, to express female spirituality and to better the world. This amazing book serves us well in offering brilliant wisdom, joyful ideas and gentle structure to our gatherings. We have been waiting for such a book, and I'm so glad it's now here. Rev. Karen Tate is a treasure – one of our most profound thinkers and doers for an ancient spirituality that is coming through just in time for all humanity. Thank you, Karen!

Rev. Ava - Founder and Presiding Priestess of the Goddess Temple of Orange County

To feel loved by the Sacred Feminine is a cure we need, and Karen Tate's Goddess Calling helps bring it forth. She offers intellectual food, intuitional inspiration and experiential nourishment to seekers on the path of restoration of the feminine principle for our world. Goddess Calling can be used as a manual to create a wisdom circle or public ritual for a holy-day. She offers words to say for the important yearly cycles of renewal of the deep feminine, as well as guided visualization meditations to take us inward to meet the world goddesses.

Reverend Tate honors the archetype of Sacred Union through the story of Mary Magdalene and returns Mary to the company of her sister goddesses where she belongs. Mary Magdalene is but one facet of the world-changing strength of the feminine spirit that comes through in this book of rituals, meditations and political perceptions.

Joan Norton *–* The Magdalene Within *and* 14 Steps to Awaken the Sacred Feminine; Women in the Circle of Mary Magdalene

Goddess Calling

Inspirational Messages and Meditations
of Sacred Feminine Liberation Thealogy

Goddess Calling

Inspirational Messages and Meditations
of Sacred Feminine Liberation Thealogy

Rev. Dr. Karen Tate

CHANGE
MAKERS
BOOKS

Winchester, UK
Washington, USA

First published by Changemakers Books, 2014
Changemakers Books is an imprint of John Hunt Publishing Ltd., Laurel House, Station Approach,
Alresford, Hants, SO24 9JH, UK
office1@jhpbooks.net
www.johnhuntpublishing.com
www.changemakers-books.com

For distributor details and how to order please visit the 'Ordering' section on our website.

Text copyright: Karen Tate 2013

ISBN: 978 1 78279 442 4

A CIP catalogue record for this book is available from the British Library.

Design: Stuart Davies

Printed and bound by CPI Group (UK) Ltd, Croydon, CR0 4YY

We operate a distinctive and ethical publishing philosophy in all
areas of our business, from our global network of authors to
production and worldwide distribution.

CONTENTS

Dedicated to

Isis – The Great She of 10,000 Names

Sekhmet – Our Lady of Tenacity Manifested

and

Roy
My Husband
The wind beneath my wings for three decades.

Other Titles by this Author

Sacred Places of Goddess: 108 Destinations
Walking an Ancient Path: Rebirthing Goddess on Planet Earth

Anthology Contributions

Waters of Life
Jesus Through Pagan Eyes
Heart of a Woman in Business
The Goddess Guide to Business Bliss

Acknowledgments

As I've been heard to say many times on my radio show, *Voices of the Sacred Feminine*, my listeners and guests are *gas in my tank* who keep me going year in and year out. Listener emails nourish and feed me, validating that what I'm doing is making a difference in their lives. My awesome guests inspire and inform, helping keep me on the cutting edge of new thought and ideas. They are not however, the only folks who sustain me. Just as Hillary Clinton showed us *it takes a village to raise a child*, I know our friends, colleagues, mentors and loved ones help us thrive, and I have been truly blessed with many generous people who have assisted me tremendously in doing what I feel called to do.

Appreciation goes out to my Sacred Sunday sisters, Shelli, Marsha, Samantha, Tony and Berit. Big hugs to my Wisdom Circle for challenging my thinking and nourishing my soul. To the Abbey of Avalon, particularly Abbess Sariel, a wise and generous woman with whom I love to bounce around my ideas, I send my admiration and love. Gina, the best webmistress I could hope to have and Cindy, my social media assistant; I couldn't do it without you both! Rev. Ava Park and the Priestesses of the Goddess Temple of Orange County, I am in awe of your decade of dedication and I thank you for being there, making herstory, and teaching me to receive. Thanks to Kris of Gaia Festival, the Green Man Store and staff, Angie and the women of Gaia's Womb, Carla and Leigh at Olandar, Emmanuel Itier of Wonderland Entertainment, Selena Fox of Circle Sanctuary, Amalya at The Goddess Studio, Rev. Loreon at Isis Oasis, Jann Aldredge-Clanton, and Rev. Stacy Boorn at Ebenezer herchurch. You have all been inspirational and supportive. Melody F. and Lauren, I couldn't manage without our evolutionary conversations. Joan N., your energy always uplifts me. David H., thank you for teaching me to be like teflon. To Jacquie,

Jenny, Alexis, Jane H., Lydia, Sabina, Meloney, Levannah, Loretta K., James R., Lora, Dharma, Liz F. and Shirley – Namaste! Marilyn and Debora W., I miss you so much!

To the women who taught the "dark goddess" or shadow lessons, you know who you are. I sincerely thank you for playing your role devised by the Great She to help me learn self-worth, boundaries and grow into my Queen archetype of leadership and service. You taught me to look for the gift in even the most cruel of circumstances and challenged me to find my true path.

To Tim Ward at Changemakers and the rest of the wonderful crew at John Hunt Publishing, including Trevor, Dielle and Stuart and everyone else who collaborated in partnership to birth this physical book into the word, I offer my heartfelt gratitude and thank you for taking another chance on me and my work!

And finally, to Roy, my husband of thirty years. I know how truly blessed I am to have you by my side doing the countless things we've shared over the years. Women in the community hold you up as an example of the ideal Goddess Husband. I doubt there's many better role models out there for what many women want and need in a partner, from the boardroom to the bedroom. You are truly the wind beneath my wings and there's no more perfect match for me than you. Thanks for being the Anubis to my Isis, at my side whether we're cruising down the Nile or choosing the seclusion of the marshlands. 143.

Rev. Dr . Karen Tate

www.karentate.com

ancientcultures@ca.rr.com

Foreword

In ever-increasing numbers women and men are seeking spirituality beyond traditional religious institutions, and more and more their new normal includes the deities, ideals and archetypes of the Sacred Feminine. They have a desire to get beyond the patriarchal dogma that often perpetuates sexism, homophobia and the domination of Gaia and all her inhabitants, including the body of Mother Earth. Women in particular are hearing and heeding their calling, stepping forth to take on their mantle of leadership as rabbis, ministers, priestesses, Nuns on the Bus and Womanpriests. They are exercising their spiritual authority in circles at their kitchen tables, in their living rooms and classrooms, in brick and mortar churches and temples, in political arenas and groves. They are flexing their spiritual wings and allowing themselves to be guided by their intuition, innate female wisdom and inner-knowing and they encourage their congregations to know and feel the essence of Goddess and understand what that new knowledge might mean for themselves personally and the world.

Often their shared message is one of female empowerment, social justice and environmental responsibility sometimes referred to as eco-feminist spirituality. The liturgy may contain social, cultural and political messages of liberation thealogy using Goddess mythology, archetypes and metaphors as benchmarks and templates for a more just and sustainable future. Gone altogether or tempered is the message of the strict authoritarian Father whose mythology gives license for a male-dominated society with women in a subordinate role. Nothing less than peace, partnership, justice, equality and care for the planet and each other are at the heart of this Sacred Feminine wisdom.

In answer to this collective call to restore and re-write our values and find a new spiritual path, women and men are blazing a trail using their pink-handled machetes to find their way. It might manifest in progressive churches using gender neutral names for God in prayer and song. Others include liturgy embracing the Divine Mother in equal partnership alongside the Father. Altars might not be dominated only by male images. Still others give themselves permission to conduct women-only services and exhibit only female images of deity at their gatherings. Congregants worship together in circles rather than in hierarchical configurations with a male intermediary between them and deity. In fact, these groups and gatherings might be leaderless, egalitarian or organizers might share leadership. In case it's not obvious, there is no one way and no absolute right way to facilitate these gatherings or to worship or interpret deity. These are just some of the new guidelines being tried across the globe as spiritual people come forward to see what works for themselves or their communities.

Yes, there has been a plethora of academic writings restoring knowledge of Goddess and women's history that has been swept beneath the rug. Some, myself included, have used this knowledge to occasionally re-construct or adapt ancient rituals for a modern context. We have gleaned inspiration from inscriptions and ancient knowledge and turned it into the seasonal ritual. Psychologists have explored the significance of Goddess archetypes. Theologians have examined why Goddess disappeared and patriarchy began to dominate. Some statistics show that when all earth-based or goddess-oriented groups are combined, Pagan, or non-Abrahamic religions are one of the fastest growing groups in the country and books have come out in equal measure to support that growing interest.

What has been missing, however, is an abundance of inspirational writings that pulls all of these aforementioned areas of focus together between two covers and puts it into an easy-to-understand and user-friendly book of sacred feminine liberation thealogy. Yes, thealogy, not theology: the meaning of Goddess, as deity, archetype and ideal and her relationship to humanity, the planet and its species. This goes beyond the wheel of the year, examining Goddess mythology and ideals of the Sacred Feminine that would reshape values, society and culture, from cradle to grave, and in pre-school to the voting booth. Goddess ideals actually do provide a template for a more just and sustainable future, and with this book, I hope I've managed to directly connect the dots between the Great She and liberation from the oppression of our patriarchal world.

This book is designed to give individuals or those desiring to serve their communities a springboard to offer what I remember were called "sermons from the pulpit" in my early days as a Catholic, with ideas to create a format for a regular gathering or service. Easy to digest and sometimes gently following the seasons of the year and holidays already on most people's calendars, these messages and meditations use Goddess archetypes, ideals and mythology to provide content for education, inspiration and contemplation for anyone seeking to incorporate a feminine face of god within their spirituality, no matter their faith – and the messages and meditations have been field-tested!

Following in one of the messages within this book, Trust in the Journey, these collective words of inspiration and guidance accumulated over time as I was called on as an ordained minister to speak about the Sacred Feminine. Yes, these messages and meditations have already been successfully shared and embraced by congregations where I have been invited to present papers, guest minister or lead salons or services for conferences, festivals, Goddess temples, Unitarian Universalist congregations, the American Academy of Religion or at Sacred Sundays, the latter being interfaith services I offered in the Los Angeles community for several years with sister-priestesses. All these experiences have provided the framework for this book and the

3

suggestions herein for readers to find personal inspiration or ready-made material to facilitate your own community circles.

As you go forward and find your sacred roar,

May Goddess Embrace You in Her Golden Wings,

Rev. Dr. Karen Tate

How to Use This Book

As I have mentioned, there is no one way to do this. What works for you and/or your group is perfect. However, I will provide a sample ritual outline with some comments which may help you begin. Feel free to be flexible, creative and adjust as you see fit.

Sources of Inspiration for the Service

When I was called upon to co-create what came to be Sacred Sunday services for the community, I turned to the format used by Unitarian Universalist congregations for inspiration. I had been invited to give talks or guest minister at a number of their church services and their format felt very accessible and simple to follow, and I am not one to try to reinvent the wheel if it's working just fine. My hope was to develop an interfaith service where people of all faiths and backgrounds would feel comfortable together.

For opening and closing music, we used our favorites, such as versions of "Ancient Mother" by Robert Gass and hymns by Jann Aldredge-Clanton who took familiar music and applied lyrics to reflect a feminine face of God. I have included a few of her songs for your use in the resources section at the end of this book. One of my favorites was "We Sound a Call to Freedom," using the melody of the "Battle Hymn of the Republic," aka "Mine Eyes Have Seen the Glory," an American folk song from the 19th century. I loved the social justice theme found in these new lyrics. Another was "Our Mother Within Us," re-written to the melody of the well-known Christmas song, "Away in a Manger." We would hand out the words to the songs or print them in a program so the congregation could sing along to these familiar melodies with or without music.

The candle-lighting portion of the outline below was inspired by the Goddess Temple of Orange County in Irvine, CA which does a much more elaborate version than what was incorporated in our services. We used a large candle with three wicks. One wick was the "divinity candle" lit in honor of the deity at the center of the service. The second wick was the "concept candle" which represented the theme of the service, such as harmony or balance. The third wick was the "perpetuation candle" lit with the intention that we would pay forward into the world that concept we were focused on and help manifest it in our lives and into the world.

The opening prayer I refer to as *We Have Forgotten Who We* Are (also called the *Prayer of Sorrow*) and the closing prayer I call *Prayer of Remembering* (also called the *Prayer of Gratitude*) came from the United Nations website under Environmental Sabbath Service, and I thank them for their permission to reprint these two prayers for this book. I felt the words captured the very essence of where we are as a species, and it was my vision that as we moved through the service, we transformed ourselves from people who have forgotten who we are to those who have remembered.

I would like to emphasize the importance of the community-sharing segment of the service. Borrowed from the Unitarian Universalist services when people came to the front of the church and shared their victories and sorrows, we quickly learned how important witnessing our congregants' sharing was for us all. The only advice I would give here is you have to be sure these sharings are concise and to the point. We expanded on the UU victories and sorrows and allowed about ten to fifteen minutes to pass a talking stick and enlist comments from the congregants about what might have come up for them as a result of the service. This encouraged a feeling of community, investment in the services and bonding among those gathered.

Some of the women who presented Sacred Sundays with me also contributed ritual ideas which we incorporated over time. My thanks goes out to Shelli who contributed her creativity, good ideas and love of fables and storytelling to the services. Together we wrote our mission statement and statement of purpose which reflected the idea we felt was important to punctuate at each service; there is no one way to worship or interpret deity. Marsha's forte was the Hindu pantheon, and she taught us mantras, traditions and practices related to those gods and goddesses which we incorporated as appropriate. Samantha came on board later and her strength was her organization, attention to detail and bringing more prayers we used as our liturgy, with an emphasis on the Wheel of the Year. Berit became our Musical Director, and we added the element of music and singing at the beginning and ending of most services.

Everyone contributed uplifting readings, affirmations, fables, and meditations that supported our monthly theme; however the ones in this book are my writings from Sacred Sunday services and various others from my many ministerial presentations. I thank these aforementioned ladies for the memorable services we facilitated as our diversity became the perfect threads that helped us weave Sacred Sundays into a beautiful tapestry of monthly services for quite some time. I also thank the other groups and congregations who offered me the opportunity to share my thoughts with their communities.

General Ritual Outline

1. Singing, chanting, drumming or sounding
2. Opening – Lighting the Temple Candle
3. Welcome
4. Statement of Purpose/Mission Statement
5. Opening Prayer: We Have Forgotten Who We Are/Prayer of Sorrow
6. Candle Lighting for Deity and/or Perpetuation of the theme/focus of your service
7. Message of Inspiration

8. Storytelling or Enactment
9. Meditation
10. Passing the Talking Stick/Community Sharing/ Announcements
11. Affirmations
12. Closing Prayer: We Remember Who We Are/Prayer of Gratitude
13. Closing song, chant or sounding
14. Extinguish the Temple Candle

WE HAVE FORGOTTEN WHO WE ARE
aka Prayer of Sorrow *

Reader: We have forgotten who we are.

We have forgotten who we are...
We have alienated ourselves from the unfolding of the cosmos
We have become estranged from the movements of the earth
We have turned our backs on the cycles of life.

Response: We have forgotten who we are.

We have sought only our own security
We have exploited simply for our own ends
We have distorted our knowledge
We have abused our power.

Response: We have forgotten who we are.

Now the land is barren
And the waters are poisoned
And the air is polluted.

Response: We have forgotten who we are.

Now the forests are dying
And the creatures are disappearing
And the humans are despairing.

Response: We have forgotten who we are.

We ask forgiveness
We ask for the gift of remembering
We ask for the strength to change.

A PRAYER OF REMEMBERING
aka Prayer of Gratitude *

Reader: **We rejoice in all life. We remember who we are.**

We live in all things.
All things live in us.

Response: We rejoice in all life. We remember who we are.

We live by the sun.
We move with the stars.

Response: We rejoice in all life. We remember who we are.

We eat from the earth.
We drink from the rain.
We breathe from the air.

Response: We rejoice in all life. We remember who we are.

We share with the creatures.
We have strength through their gifts.

Response: We rejoice in all life. We remember who we are.

We depend on the forests.
We have knowledge through their secrets.

Response: We rejoice in all life. We remember who we are.

We have the privilege of seeing and understanding.
We have the responsibility of caring.
We have the joy of celebrating.

Reader: We rejoice in all life. We remember who we are.

Prayer of Sorrow and *Prayer of Gratitude* reprinted with permission as found in "Only One Earth," a United Nations Environment Programmer publication for "Environmental Sabbath/Earth Rest Day," New York, June 1990

Messages

Some of the messages might lend themselves to natural cycles of Mother Earth or coincide with a particular time of the year, such as using the *Resolutions* and *Return of the Light* message in January, but all of the messages are designed to use anytime. You will find that some of the messages suggest exercises or enactments that might be done during the service.

Meditations

Meditations are designed to sometimes be coordinated with particular messages and usually employ Goddess imagery helping the person meditating accomplish something: healing, transformation, manifestation. Meditations are also designed to assist in achieving a quality, virtue or state of mind: courage and strength, dreaming and inspiration, self-worth and true beauty. When doing the meditations, particularly if you are an individual adapting this book for yourself, you might want to consider recording the meditation, then playing it back for yourself. You might also do that for group meditations and provide a little mood music in the background.

Songs

Two songs from Jann Aldredge Clanton are provided in the end matter of the book. Occasionally we took the liberty of changing a word or two depending on our congregation such as in switching the lyrics of "Christ-Sophia" for "Goddess" when more appropriate. If you don't read music, you can find these melodies on the internet.

Part I

The Politics of Eco-Feminist Goddess Spirituality – A Theology for a Sustainable Future[1]

Goddess is a Democrat! Imagine the feedback from that statement from interviews with notable leaders in the political and spiritual community on my radio show, *Voices of the Sacred Feminine!* But what were we really saying in that statement that might not have been immediately evident? We were saying the strategy to move us toward that paradigm shift, into a post-kyriarchal world, would not just be the use of secular law, but a change in thealogy. We believe at the Institute for Thealogy and Deasophy, as do many others, that the mythology of the Sacred Feminine, deity, archetype and ideal, might reestablish the foundations on our planet necessary for a sustainable future for all life and Mother Earth.

Here's the line of thought. We know religion, law, and society are shaped in large part by our mythology. We believe the ancient mythology of the Sacred Feminine, perhaps 40,000 years old or more, has been obscured and demonized, particularly in the West, by Abrahamic traditions' immature-youngster-male-dominated religions, linchpins of patriarchy, leaving us with false normalcy. This results in cultures that set men above women, with men indoctrinated to believe they are the rightful masters over Nature and intolerant male-dominated religions believing their god is the only real god who gives them license to crusade against non-believers. Having nothing to counter this unnatural imbalance, we have been left to endure all manner of oppression: fundamentalism, genocide, militarism, imperialism, homophobia, racism, infanticide, sexism, female genital mutilation, predator capitalism, slavery, exploitation, corporate fascism and threats to our democracy. All this we face, in conjunction with potential environmental catastrophe that can effect national security and life on the planet as we know it. According to Egyptian feminist and professor, Nawal El Saadawi, "Patriarchy needs god to justify injustice."[2] Therefore, until we can get religion out of politics and economics, Goddess advocates counter we must start rethinking our mythology, or our religion.

We must see the Divine not just in male terms, which is dominant in the collective psyche. We must also see the Divine in female terms and value the ideals that go along with maternal values, or we may never achieve a contemporary egalitarian society of equality, partnership, and peace for people of Gaia.

Compare the generally accepted views of liberals and conservatives. Peter Michaelson, psychoanalytic psychotherapist and author, in his article, "The Primitive Conservative Psyche,"[3] extrapolates from the insights of Berkeley professor of linguistics and cognitive science, George Lakoff, in his article, "What Conservatives Really Want."[4] According to Michaelson, citing Lakoff, the conservative belief in individual responsibility to the exclusion of social responsibility is based on the model of the strict authoritarian father, sometimes called the psychological or Freudian super ego or inner critic, which can manifest in the weak or unaware mind as judgmental, aggressive, negative, ruthless, mocking, unforgiving and irrational, with a distrust of government. Michaelson equates conservative mentality to a primitive aspect of human nature explaining "Conservatives' mental gymnastics for disrespecting the poor enable them to practice guilt-free ruthlessness while feeling morally superior...." They rationalize their lack of empathy by claiming that the poor deserve their poverty because they are responsible for their own failings rather than considering they might be doing well considering the hand they've been dealt. Likewise we observe many conservative Christians who misinterpret doctrine believing their wealth as a gift from God for their discipline and rationalize poverty as punishment for sin or being lazy.[5] A vast majority of conservatives tend to want to support established institutions for social stability even if this stable order means the oppression of patriarchy. According to economist John Kenneth Galbraith, "The modern conservative is engaged in one of man's oldest exercises in moral philosophy; that is, the search for a superior moral justification for selfishness."[6]

On the flip side, according to Webster's dictionary, liberals are generous, broad-minded, tolerant and believe in individual rights and freedom.[7] Politically, liberals desire progress and value equality, diversity and social justice. They view government as the protector of the environment and people and want government to help alleviate social ills and protect civil liberties and human rights.[8] That said, perhaps it is clear to see why community leaders and activists, along with many other Goddess advocates, have said that **until we have a viable Eco-Feminist-Goddess-like political party**, maternal values of the Sacred Feminine are more in sync with liberal and progressive ideals, which are the home of the true Democratic party.

So let us look at several examples of the marriage between liberal values, political platforms of Democrats, and Sacred Feminine mythology.

We find, under the broad umbrella of Goddess, many faces across continents and cultures, with no mandate that we worship one name, one face. Instead we see a metaphor for plurality, diversity and inclusion in the loving and life-affirming Sacred Feminine, rather than the jealous, One Way, androcentric and exclusionary god of patriarchy keen on asking men to sacrifice their sons to prove their loyalty and a holy book filled with violence.[9]

Likewise, the Democratic umbrella casts its net wide. Generally speaking, it is the natural home of those embracing gender equality and peoples of all walks of life: gay, straight, people of all skin colors and religions or no religion at all. Juxtapose that with the majority of white, Christian faces peering out at you from a male-dominated Republican National Convention.

Consider the mythology of the Inuit Goddess Sedna. She is the gatekeeper between humankind and the sea creatures upon which people depend for their livelihood. If mankind becomes too greedy and exploits the creatures of the sea, Sedna cuts him off until he takes only what he needs. Greed and excess are taboo as we are all inter-dependent upon each other.

Likewise, **real Democrats**, not Blue Dog Dems or Clintonian corporatists, are the gatekeepers demanding regulation so that corporations cannot run amok and destroy the resources of Mother Earth or rights of people. Most notable is former Vice President Al Gore who, having pressed for stern regulation of greenhouse gases, won the Nobel Peace Prize for his efforts to build greater knowledge about man-made climate change. On the other hand, because of the Republican world view in favor of free trade and globalization, the GOP has fought against taking steps to alleviate the threat of climate change. They dismiss it as a hoax or socialist plot to redistribute wealth from corporate polluters to the poor nations they've harmed, and they support their corporate constituents who pour billions of dollars into keeping the public misinformed.

The Egyptian Goddess Isis bestowed upon pharaohs their right to rule, and they were to rule their kingdoms under the laws of the Goddess Ma'at, namely truth, balance, order, and justice. Likewise the Roman Lady Libertas represented the deification of the virtue of freedom.

It should be noted that it was under Democratic administrations that progress was made on civil rights and social safety nets while Republicans generally put corporate interests before people, case in point the Conservative leaning Supreme Court's decision that corporations are people which has had a disastrous effect on the democratic process. Republicans have forced a watering down of regulation of Wall Street and threaten to defund many consumer protections agencies. And how can we ignore Fox News, arm of the Republican Party, that cannot get into Canada because of regulations there against the media disseminating misinformation.[10]

In the thealogy of the Sacred Feminine, Goddess affirms women's bodies and sexuality. Priestesses of pharmacology, midwives and women hold the power over their own bodies, and life and death is in their hands.

Today the patriarchy dictates to women the parameters of beauty, and women fall victims to their standards spending millions with plastic surgeons to live up to some impossible ideal. According to the American Society of Plastic Surgeons, 13.1 million cosmetic procedures were performed in 2010, up 5% from 2009. Beyond physical beauty, the patriarchy wants to control all aspects of women's sexuality and reproduction. Known in the United States as Big Pharma, pharmaceutical companies now hold the power over women's bodies as they encourage women to disconnect from their menses, that monthly inconvenience, that curse. They say, "Here, take our pill and see your sacred blood magically disappear. Disconnect from one of the very things that empowers you as a woman!" In a not-so veiled and on-going culture war, the GOP has declared war on women by attempting to de-fund Planned Parenthood, thwart access to contraception, pass laws to make divorces harder to obtain, legalize the murder of abortion providers, have miscarriages investigated and abortions abolished. Women's bodies and lives are the terrain on which this current extremist conservative movement has been taking a stand since Barack Obama has been elected President of the United States.

Goddess thealogy affirms female power. Where Goddess was worshiped, her temples were the centers of wisdom, culture, and financial power and were often presided over by women. Researchers such as Merlin Stone and Heide Goettner-Abendroth, in her book, *Societies of Peace: Matriarchies Past, Present and Future,* point to matriarchal societies where Goddess was venerated and maternal values practiced; women and children were protected and had a spot at the center of the culture, reaping the benefit of that positioning.

According to activist and psychiatrist Nawal El Saadawi, there can be no real democracy without equality, and there is neither under patriarchy. Fortunately, the strides made by the United Nations, the U.S. State Department, and outspoken way-showers help to empower women. Case in point, former President and Democrat Jimmy Carter, left the Southern Baptist Church and declared very publicly it was because of how the Bible discriminates against the female gender and thwarts women from realizing their fullest potential. Fathers Roy Bourgeois and Matthew Fox were both excommunicated by the Vatican for their very public pro-feminine positions. Feminist women are at the forefront exploring "exchange and gift economics" as an antidote to crumbling capitalism. This very empowerment is considered by many to be the moral imperative of our time.

Conversely, Republicans continue to vote down laws that would guarantee equal pay for women despite women being heads of households.[11] According to UN Women citing UNICEF, women perform 66% of the world's work, produce 50% of the food, but earn 10% of the income and own 1% of the property.[12] *The White House Project Report: Benchmarking Women's Leadership* found females comprise only 23% of leadership positions within academia, 16% within corporations, 17% in politics and 15% in religious institutions.[13] When all sectors were averaged, we have only 18% of women in leadership positions overall – hardly the needed critical mass to influence the direction of our country or society. In America alone more than three million elderly women live in poverty and the typical woman working full time, all year, earns just 77% of what her male counterpart earns.[14] Writing for *The Nation* magazine in the article titled "The War on Women's Futures," Princeton professor and author, Melissa Harris Perry, decodes the message shrouded in the language of Republican fiscal austerity which disproportionately affects women. She cites the GOP's social agenda unravels the progress made by women, forcing them back into the domestic sphere as they cut family planning services, creating an environment of compulsory childbearing where women can't control their fertility. This makes it more difficult for women to compete for degrees or jobs with their male counterparts.[15]

Within Goddess spirituality or religion, advocates believe we do not diminish other men and women to assert our own strength. We do not exploit others. We strive for win-win situations through negotiation and partnerships, not power over and domination.

Over the years we have witnessed how patriarchy, militarism, imperialism, colonialism, conquest, and fundamentalism exploit people and resources creating poverty and inequity at home and across the globe. We can witness how predator or disaster capitalism is used to amass great wealth and grab power for the Haves, leaving the Have Nots vulnerable and at a disadvantage. We see how the absence of journalistic integrity coupled with corporate interests can result in a country brainwashed into any number of ideas, including the bogus Iraq war ginned up by the Bush administration. Anyone going to the George W. Bush library in Texas will hear a rewriting of the history of 9-11 and the Iraq war. We see how history and school books are rewritten to serve a conservative agenda. We see in California how Tier One religions (Protestant, Catholic, Jewish, Muslim and Native American) have rights and protections not afforded Tier Two religions, as in the case of Chaplain Patrick McCollum's legal struggle with the state of California.[16] We fear how the current economic, environmental and political crises we face will be exploited to militarize our societies and further strip away rights and liberties.

We are standing at the crossroads with the Goddess Hecate. She is shining her light and showing us where we have been, where we are, and where we might go. It is up to us to decide what kind of world we want to live in. Mahatma Gandhi was asked by a journalist what he thought of Western civilization. He answered, "It would be a good idea".[17] Will mankind try to practice civilization?

We say we are a religious nation, yet the poverty rate is the third worst among developed nations according to the Organization for Economic Cooperation and Development, and the poverty rate is expected to rise from 13.2 percent to 15 percent this year.[18] Forty million Americans are on food stamps and that number is also expected to rise.[19] 99ers, those people whose unemployment benefits ran out long ago, are off everyone's radar screen. Yet despite unemployment benefits being an insurance workers pay into, Republicans held these benefits hostage until President Obama agreed to extend tax cuts for the richest 2% of people in the country. The GOP/Republicans are not even making an attempt to pretend they're interested in creating jobs despite that being their rhetoric to get elected in 2010. Since President Obama has been in the White House they have spent all their time voting to repeal the Affordable Care Act providing healthcare to millions of uninsured, though it was originally a Republican idea bringing many new customers to the healthcare industry, rather than a single-payer, medicare-like option most liberals wanted. To date, they have voted to repeal it 40 times. The GOP-dominated House of Representatives has done little else besides name libraries, vote against measures that might provide some regulation on the purchase of assault weapons, vote for blocking women's rights to their own bodies and against justice in the workplace. House Republican leader, John Boehner, famous for passing out checks from tobacco lobbyists on the floor of Congress, said if their budget cuts cost Americans more jobs, "So be it"[20] while the National Law Center on Homelessness and Poverty estimates that 700,000 to 2 million people are homeless on any given night.[21] In early 2011, the Republican Governor of Michigan, Rick Snyder, was trying to pass a law to take money directly from the poor and elderly, and he did not even try to hide the fact he planned to give it to corporations instead.[22] In a war on democracy, he also wanted to pass a law that would allow him to dismiss elected officials and turn over the running of cities to corporations if the city was deemed in financial crisis. Time has shown how this disproportionately affects African American communities.[24] Several Republican governors are destroying Labor's right to collective bargaining.[24] We are the only industrialized nation that doesn't provide healthcare for all its citizens. Republicans, the so-called family values folk, want to keep us at the mercy of healthcare monopolies. The latest census figures show the gap between rich and poor widening to the largest margin ever with the richest 1 percent pockets more than 20 percent of total income which is greater than the total amount earned by the bottom 50 percent.[25] CEOs that once made about 25 times more than their employees now make 350 times more than workers.[26] Almost three years after the melt down on Wall Street, few executives have been criminally charged while Main Street suffers.[27] And Republicans continue to roll back progress or thwart bills and laws that protect citizens, like progress made for clean air, food safety and healthcare.

After President Obama defeated Republican presidential hopeful, Mitt Romney, by a landslide, the GOP said publicly they must expand their tent if they wanted to win another national election, but rather than actually offer policies that benefit the 99%, they have instead used the activist and conservative-leaning Supreme Court, along with GOP-controlled State governments, to dismantle laws that protect voting rights, which adversely affect African Americans, students, the poor and elderly – all voting groups usually lining up under the banner of the Democrats. Within hours of the Supreme Court tossing out voting laws that had been on the books for decades, many states were busy finding an assortment of ways to make voting harder for potential Democratic-leaning voters. We will have to see what ramifications this strategy will have in the coming elections of 2014 and 2016 if the federal government cannot prevent this voter suppression.

The Dalai Lama said it would be Western women who would come to the rescue of the world.[28] Might it actually be Goddess Thealogy? How would people react to a change in the mythology? Well, if the popularity of the recent movie *Avatar* is any indicator, the movie many I know equated with *Goddess church*, I think the Sacred Feminine might stage a coup based on the concept of inter-connection, reverence for Nature, a Mother Goddess, and respect of one another and the planet. Most people thought those were pretty cool ideas they would like practiced in society. My radio show listeners proclaimed they wanted to book passage on the first ship to Pandora! Over and over people in my community, with teary eyes, retold the powerful scene in Avatar as Jake knelt at the Tree of Souls, imploring Pandora's Goddess for help, saying his race, the Earthlings, called the Sky People, had destroyed their Mother and tomorrow they were coming to destroy Her. Perhaps due to such a positive and enthusiastic public response to the movie, the Vatican felt it needed to chime in with their warning. Vatican spokesman, Rev. Federico Lombardi reiterated Pope Benedict XVI's views on the dangers of turning nature into a "new divinity."[29] And yes, many conservative evangelical Christians saw no value in Pandora's ideals. All over the internet readers could see many preferred a military conquest and corporate victory over The Other – you know, people not like them, those blue-skinned tree huggers.[30]

Well, the tree huggers on Gaia, people of all colors, genders and religions are calling on Goddess Thealogy to reset the balance as she did on Pandora. Can we do it? Can change happen?

When St. Paul was run out of Ephesus, lucky to be alive after he tried to turn the masses away from their beloved Goddess Artemis, he must have wondered if this fledgling Christianity he was selling would ever stick. If you lived and worshiped in Pagan Rome, you probably never dreamed you would see the day the empire would be dominated by Christians, and if you were an early Christian fearing for your life, you surely wondered what the future held. Women being burned at the stake during the Inquisition surely could not foresee the changes that might be in store for women, no doubt like their sisters of the nineteenth century, when it was debated if women had souls. Slavery was the norm across the globe in ancient times, including in the fledgling United States. Contemporary films like *Iron Jawed Angels* have documented how American women fighting for the vote were abused and threatened with institutionalization and arrest for their activism and desire for equality.[31] It has only been in the last few decades that African American men could play in the professional baseball league. Certainly, not that long ago, the thought of an African American or woman becoming President was unheard of in the United States; yet now, many are saying Hillary Clinton will certainly follow President Obama to the Oval Office and become the nation's first female President.

One thing is certain, change and transformation are inevitable. They occur when enough people will it, usually after a profound event, or when circumstances collide that usher in transitions of new beginnings. Recent events, whether across the globe, as in the Arab Spring in Egypt and the struggles in Syria, or closer to home, with the partisan political battle to retain worker rights in Wisconsin or the occupation of Wall Street and Washington D.C., or food industry workers demanding a living minimum wage of $15.00 an hour, people from all walks of life are responding. They are beginning to organize at home and abroad and respond to the naked greed, the rape of the environment, voter oppression, swelling poverty, disaster capitalism, abuses of Wall Street, inequality and injustice, threats to their social safety nets, austerity measures, unemployment, jobs being shipped overseas, and the regressive politics of Republicans so obviously not inter-ested in helping anyone but corporations. But have the majority of people had enough yet? Can these social and political activists tip the scales in favor of the Have Nots? Will values of the Sacred Feminine finally have their rightful place in society? Will Goddess Thealogy be reborn in the mainstream world?

Gaia, Kali, Sekhmet, Isis, Durga, Ma'at, Sedna, Libertas, Demeter – we call upon you to help us reset the balance! Ginestho! Let it be done!

Part II

Messages

Chapter 1

Resolutions and Return of the Light

Welcome friends, not just to today's service, but to the New Year! If you are familiar with Goddess or earth-based spirituality, you no doubt know or have been hearing for over a month about the Winter Solstice and the returning of the light. We have heard that our northern European ancestors called the holiday of Winter Solstice Mother's Night, when the female ancestors and Goddess were celebrated and their guidance sought out by the people. We know it is the time to celebrate the Roman God, Saturn, as well as Mithras and Jesus. We tell tales of the Yuletide Goddesses such as Lucia and Holda and how the Druids celebrated their "festival of liberation," a time when the soul is set free to dream a new world. The returning of the light from Winter Solstice forward for a time is not just about whether we see more darkness or light in the sky. The light actually symbolizes the potential for life and new beginnings.

That said, let me share a little story with you with a new perspective on the season, a myth I don't think gets so much play at this time of year. It's about the Sun Goddess, Amaterasu, a Shinto Goddess, whose sacred sites are on the island of Japan.

Her myth shares similarities to the Greek Goddess, Demeter, and her bawdy and unrestrained counterpart, Baubo. You see, in her sorrow, Amaterasu, like Demeter, withdrew from the world causing the land to become barren and bleak. In her grief, Amaterasu secluded herself in a cave. No amount of coaxing could get Amaterasu to come out and restore fertility and vegetation to the land. Until, like in the story of Demeter and Baubo, Amaterasu was also coaxed out of hiding and despair by her counterpart in the myth, Uzume. Legend has it Amaterasu peeked out from the cave, her curiosity aroused by the laughter

28

and clapping inspired by Uzume's dance – but this wasn't just any dance. You see, like Baubo, Uzume was "lifting her skirt," a nice euphemism for showing her genitals or yoni!

Why? You might ask. Well, on the exoteric level, it might seem funny or lewd to watch someone dance an erotic dance, or strip tease, if you will. I can't forget the woman on the stage popping ping pong balls from her yoni in the movie, *Priscilla, Queen of the Desert*, the curious Japanese men holding their mini-flashlights hoping to get a glimpse of the yoni of female performers spreading their knees on stage. The yoni then and now holds great power and mystery. These stories of the dances of Baubo and Uzume are not meant to be lewd. They are, in fact, meant to be sacred. They are from a time when procreation and sexual union were still considered sacred and sex had not yet become something shameful or taboo. A woman's body held the mysteries of the cycles of life and death. You might recall those sacred statues in museums highlighting the pubic triangle, that part of the woman's body known to be the gateway or threshold of fertility and new life – until Christianity turned what was normal, natural and sacred on its head!

Baubo and Uzume's yoni dances were the catalysts jump-starting Demeter and Amaterasu to once again spark new life. Think about the last time you really had a belly-laugh. Did you not feel alive and vital? Seeing the dances of their counterparts brought Amaterasu and Demeter such joy that life was rekindled. Vegetation sprang forth once more, and humanity could once again eat, sustain itself. People and creatures would live and not starve.

In the story of Amaterasu, it is also said that as she peeked from the cave to look upon Uzume's dance, she caught sight of her own image in a bronze mirror, and as she became dazzled by her own radiance, light and fertility were restored to the world. Some scholars believe this myth reflects the regenerative force. It is the power and awe inspired by the yoni across cultures as a catalyst for creation, change, healing or protection. Let us remember also that women, as life-givers, were associated with Goddess, herself, the Creatrix of the world and everything in the universe. Life springs forth from women's bodies, and women bleed without dying. This is very powerful magic. Simply put, without the yonis in these stories, without the yonis in our stories, life ceases to exist. Specific to the Sun Goddess, Amaterasu's story, and in many other spiritual traditions, as well as in science and nature, there is usually *no life without light*.

That brings us back to this season of the returning of the light. The days and nights are of equal length with the days continuing to build in length and the nights shortening until the Summer Solstice in June. We too are coming out of the darkness and building momentum and energy, or gathering light within ourselves, to do things and to manifest our desires in the world.

If we are in sync with the cosmic forces, this is the time for our own awakening and transformation and our evolution as people and spiritual beings. Each turning of the wheel at this time of the year enables us to renew ourselves, be who we always hoped we'd be and hopefully see things more clearly as we grow in wisdom. We have more juice now to re-invent ourselves, if you will. The light helps us see the world and ourselves more clearly and our role in the cosmic dance. Light shines forth, offering illumination that might give us clues to our destiny and purpose in life. This is the time that we take the ideas and seeds we planted in the dark fertile ground of winter and nurture them to burst forth in the world.

So with all that explained, can you see why this is the time of year when we make resolutions? Can you see how that tradition is based on actual natural, cosmic and spiritual laws? Let us use this time to fill our vessel with the light that nourishes our potential and fills us with life and with incentive to accomplish positive change.

I would be remiss while we are talking about light and motivation to not mention the Goddess or Saint, Brigid of Ireland. She is both fire Goddess and Goddess of the healing waters. What do you get when you mix heat and water? STEAM! And what's steam? Steam is a force that propels you forward. Think too of Brigid's steam as a catalyst around this time of year that helps us renew ourselves, transform and succeed in the resolutions we make.

You have the natural energies of the universe working with you in these months leading up to Summer Solstice to see your resolutions through. Here are a few suggestions to help you accomplish your goals: Make sure your resolution is reasonable. Do not try to make more than one change at a time. Tie a string to your wrist to act as a trigger to keep you focused on your goal. Have a deadline to accomplish that goal and a plan how you're going to accomplish your resolution. Do research or enlist help if you need it to assure success. Keep a diary of your progress, challenges and success. Show gratitude for your accomplishments!

So as we go forward, it's also important to remember our thoughts are powerful tools of manifestation, so nurture your attitude and thoughts with love. We must be the change we want to see in the world, cliché as that might sound. We must **resolve** to live our lives according to how we would like to see society change. So as we look within and outside ourselves, let us be filled with a certainty that the light will shine forth in the coming months providing transparency, healing, balance and enlightenment not just to ourselves but to humanity. Let us ride this roller-coaster of a paradigm shift not white-knuckled and in fear, but resolute to be filled with hope and excitement for the new world we can create together.

Chapter 2

Dreaming and Inspiration

The tiny Maltese islands, located just south of Sicily, are home to the oldest megalithic freestanding stone structures that exist on Earth today and designated UNESCO World Heritage Sites. These intriguing structures, many of which resemble the shape of a woman's body, predate the Egyptian pyramids and Stonehenge. One famous artifact found in these ancient sacred sites, the Sleeping Lady, is thought to be representative of the Goddess religion practiced on the islands. Discovered in the enormous underground, labyrinth-like structure called the Hal Saflieni Hypogeum, which might have once been a sanctuary and later a necropolis, the Sleeping Lady is as much of an enigma as the location in which she was found.

Because of amateur and shoddy archaeological practices being employed at the time the Sleeping Lady was found, definitive scientific evidence is lacking about the exact nature and purpose of both The Sleeping Lady and the Hypogeum, but many theories abound. Having visited several of these woman-shaped temples, as well as the underground Hypogeum, I can personally attest to the sacred energetic that still exists among the ancient stone structures which seem to activate an intuitive remembering. This is particularly true within the womb-like Hypogeum, built in the fourth millennia and composed of three underground stories. One is flooded with emotions being within this incredible holy site, particularly when the ethereal echoes of sound begins to reverberate within the space. While some believe the Hypogeum was used as a tomb or to practice the chthonic mysteries of Goddess, the suggestion of the pose of the Sleeping Lady leads many to believe this was a sacred place used for the ancient healing art of dream incubation. This was an early healing modality where the divine would intercede and lend guidance or inspiration while the subject was asleep.

The Sleeping Lady of Malta found within the Hypogeum was hardly the only example of ancient mortal and divine inter-action. That inner voice, that divine guidance, those whispers that inspire us to act or create, entered the psyche of our ancestors in various ways. In ancient times these messages arrived in a dream via a disembodied voice or in a vision. In the Old and New Testament, these dreams of divine self-disclosure were called visions of the night. Physical appearances or manifestations of a deity were events of theophany or an epiphany. Ideas of divine guidance or revelation might also be called epiphanies.

In writing to their congregations, we have evidence of Apostles who have had visions of Goddess while they were awake. In Greece, Asklepios and Hygeia, God and Goddess of Healing, were seen in visionary dreams by those who came to healing temples for treatment using the aforementioned ancient healing art of dream incubations. After fasting and purification rites, the sick would sleep in the temple overnight in hope of receiving divine guidance to cure what ailed them. Dream incubation was also practiced in sacred temples by the Chinese. Native Americans went on dream quests where they would go out into the wilderness, fast and pray as a rite of passage, and in doing so, hopefully receive divine guidance. The ancient Egyptians also believed through the power of dreams they might receive messages from their many gods and goddesses. The Dreamtime is an integral component of the culture of the Australian Aboriginal tribes who believe the connection between the physical world and spiritual consciousness is reached during dreaming. These dreams shed light on their own inner landscape, as well as inform about ancestors, history, fate, and culture in the past, present and future, simultaneously.

With the onset of science, and our disconnection with Nature, less and less faith and belief has been put in such methods. Today, occurrences of divine dreams and visions might be seen as unimportant and silly. They could be viewed as flights of fancy, neurosis, hallucinations, or as wish-fulfilling. And with some patriarchal religions rarely encouraging this personally empowered direct link to the Divine Source, or the divine knowledge of gnosis, such methods might at best be discouraged and doubted, or at worst, feared and interpreted as evil. It has been well documented what obstacles must be overcome before an apparition is accepted as real by the Vatican.

Could it be too many of us have stopped believing in dreams and visions? Perhaps we may have consequently severed or weakened that vital link to our God/dess Self or that gnosis that lies buried within. Many people do not attempt to remember their dreams or give any credence to these glimpses we are given. Could we have gotten too sophisticated and "big for our britches?" Might our ancestors, in a simpler time, have been more in touch with the Divine?

In more contemporary times, The Sleeping Prophet, Edgar Cayce, was famous the world over for his dream interpretations. He once said, "Dreams, visions, impressions, to the entity in the normal sleeping state, are the presentations of the experiences necessary for the development, if the entity would apply them in the physical life. These may be taken as warnings, as advice, as conditions to be met, conditions to be viewed in a way and manner as lessons, as truths, as they are presented in the various ways and manners." Cayce believed the information he received in these dreams was from two sources: the subconscious mind of the individual for whom he was giving a reading and the etheric source of information called the Akashic Records, a sort of universal database for every thought, word, or deed that has transpired in the past, present and future.

On the other hand, Sigmund Freud theorized that dreams were a reflection of human desires and were prompted by external stimuli. He and Carl Jung believed dreams were the interaction between the unconscious and the conscious. Psychologist Joe Griffin believed dreams were metaphorical translations of waking expectations not acted upon during the day to quell their arousal. He believed dreaming deactivated the emotional arousal, freeing the brain to be fresh each day...sort of like cleaning one's palate between taste tests. Carl Sagan considered dreams neurological waste products with little subjective significance or meaning; however he believed REM sleep serves an important survival function in that being deprived of this state more than five days can cause hallucinations. Many psychologists believe dreams can help humans understand their subconscious thought processes in an attempt to overcome psychological difficulties. Contemporary researchers in the fields of dream work and parapsychology are once again using dream incubation techniques as they revive the ancient healing practice.

There is no definitive answer on dreams, whether they might be divinely inspired or not, if they can aid in predicting the future or healing the sick, or if they give insight into our own psyches, or provide a direct connection to the Source. Perhaps the best approach is not to question too critically this source of creativity, inspiration, vision and imagination, or any safe means that allows for personal growth and illumination. We can look to dreams for insight and contemplate the messages yet never relinquish our free will to make our own decisions without turning off the flow from the spigot.

Good advice comes from Carol Koleman when writing about Yhi, Goddess of Light and Creation. She states, "To bring life to the myriad of future creations waiting within, we must first acknowledge their absolute existence and believe that we can make them emerge through our own efforts. Remember there is magical possibility in every crevice of the cave! It only waits for our light to release it. If we ponder the gifts of our ancestors and honor the blessings we have now, the internal and external landscape of our world will be lush with life."

Chapter 3

Our Messiah – She of Ten Thousand Names

Within Judeo-Christian tradition, Palm Sunday traditionally commemorates the triumphal entry of Jesus into Jerusalem to celebrate the Passover. The gospels record the arrival of Jesus riding into the city on a donkey, while the crowds spread their cloaks and palm branches on the street to honor him as their long-awaited Messiah and King. But long before the new religion of Christianity arose, the Great Mother was celebrated in the ancient world at this season of Spring by carrying in procession the branches of palms, pines and other trees. Herstory records a Creatrix and Messiah, She of Ten Thousand Names, far, far older than the deities of Judaism, Christianity, Islam and other more recent religions.

So this morning, I humbly take on the role of contemporary bard and prophetess to reclaim the Herstory, of the long-awaited return of the Great She, Goddess, our female Messiah of Ten Thousand Names, and we will together vision the prophecies attached to that coming.

How might life be different with the Divine Feminine or Goddess birthed at the center of the world, particularly for women and our like-minded brothers, without the domination of patriarchy's clenched fists?

Ah but wait. That is the end of the tale, isn't it? To understand how things have come to be so turned upside-down, let us start at the place where every good bard starts their telling of what came to pass. Let us start at the beginning.

As many of you know from the artifacts of her devoted, Goddess was revered on this planet we call Gaia, as much as 40,000 years ago, long before a male god, which is a relatively new invention. Gaia, our great Creatrix, brought forth all we needed to sustain ourselves so that life might take hold and thrive. We believe women were revered because they brought forth new life. They were seen as powerful. They could bleed without dying, and this was magical, indeed!

Women watched and learned from Mother Nature. They began to understand how Goddesses like Demeter gave us the seed, and women soon birthed the skills of agriculture. From the Mistress of the Animals, they learned animal husbandry. They used her plants to heal the sick, help bring babies into the world, thus becoming the first doctors and pharmacologists, holding life and death in their hands. They brought forth from their sacred yonis new life. Communities began to flourish, and art, music and dancing was born.

In many places women were primary or lived in peaceful egalitarian societies with men. Just like today, women were the glue that held the family units and communities together. We know marriage was not always required, and children were raised by the women and uncles of the tribe. Women passed their authority and assets down through their daughters, and men were granted power through the Goddess or Queen. Goddesses like Themis and Athena brought us law and wisdom; Libertas and Kali, social justice; and Sedna, environmentalism and a warning against greed and exploitation. Goddess myths taught us everything we needed to know to thrive in balance on the planet and with each other. And yes, Goddess was celebrated across continents and cultures. Women baked Cakes for the Queen of Heaven. They offered up piglets at the temples of Demeter and Persephone, or incense and wine were sacrificed to Artemis. Boats laden with precious offerings were launched into the sea to honor Isis. And in Rome at this time of year, we know of the Festival of The Entry of the Tree, when clergy of Magna Mater, the Great Mother, also known as Cybele, carried pine or palm trees and their branches through the city to celebrate her. As with so many Christian practices like Palm Sunday, their origins were co-opted from already existing Pagan beliefs and rituals.

But soon, in many different places, over much time and for many reasons, patriarchy was born, and this time of peace and prosperity would not last. You see, people began to think of the I and the Me instead of the Us and the We. They began to think of growing their personal property at the expense of others and Mother Earth, instead of our collective well-being. They took woman, the animals and the earth to be their possessions, their chattel. And there was great suffering across all the lands, to this day!

And with this shift, this great *gendercide*, life as we knew it came to pass. Along with the marginalizing of woman, adversaries of the Sacred Feminine tried to sweep away awareness and knowledge of Goddess for all time – and with that sweeping away, when the Great She was made to disappear because of the religion of selfish and disconnected men and their war gods, women and their power, their leadership, and their natural spiritual authority were thwarted, repressed, diminished and disrespected and became taboo. And the men, they suffered too.

We know if a culture reveres a war god, that culture will be a warrior culture. If that culture has only male leadership, that culture will be dominated by men. And thus it was for thousands of years: imbalance, injustice, abomination.

Women, once considered sacred, the Earth, once seen as sacred, the animals once seen as gifts from She of Ten Thousand Names, all became commodities of the patriarchy, of the authoritarian Father, rather than the nurturing, life affirming, compassionate Mother. Not that long ago, it was questioned if women even had souls, and their wombs were no more than an incubator for the male seed. Yes, there was a great sadness upon the land and among her peoples because only a few at the top reaped the benefit of all the resources on Mother Earth. The rest were left scraping by, fighting for the crumbs at the bottom of the heap.

So how did that manifest itself for women in everyday life?

What are the consequences of sweeping away the Great She? What happens when women are no longer equal and associated with the Divine Mother?

I share with you these inhumanities against the Feminine on this planet:

Domestic violence and sexual abuse is rampant, including the barbarity of female genital mutilation, or FGM, where a woman's sacred yoni is cut with a sharpened shell or knife so that her sexuality might be controlled because, with this mutilation, she cannot enjoy sex. Yes, this abomination happens even here in the United States leaving women with physical and emotional suffering for a lifetime!

Seventy percent of women retire in poverty after a life time of institutionalized discrimination in the workplace without equal pay or compensation for staying home to care for their families.

Women's leadership is thwarted. While being the majority gender in our country, there is less than 20% representation by women in Congress, corporations, religious institutions and academia. Millions of children go to bed hungry in the United States, and working families and seniors live in poverty. White women are paid only 74 cents on the dollar, compared to men, and less if they are Hispanic or Black. Yet, Republicans continue to refuse to pass pro-women legislation, including Equal Pay for Equal Work legislation, and only reluctantly passed the Violence Against Women Act, lest they face public humiliation. Women and children are at the margins of societies the world over suffering from the worst health care, education and human rights.

Bride-burning and arranged marriages still exist. Women may be shunned from families or seen to bring shame to their family if they have been raped or believed to have committed adultery. Tragic consequences for them can include being stoned to death or having acid thrown in the face for disobeying male authority. Girls' schools are fire-bombed by fundamentalists.

Patriarchy's largely unattainable view of beauty has created millions of women with eating disorders, flocking to cosmetic surgeons. Distorted views of women and sexuality result in an obsessive and unhealthy pornography industry or disrespectful displays from the media. Case in point, the recent female denigrating, male-dominated Academy Awards show with top male actors singing in the opening skit about women's *boobs*. Human trafficking, aka slavery and forced prostitution, are profound problems across the globe. Rape is used as a weapon of war. Some Republican congressmen even believe if you're raped, you must have "asked for it" because certainly "legitimate rape" will not result in an unwanted pregnancy.

Women are being duped by the Evangelical "new feminism" that encourages submissiveness and dependence. In groups like the Quiverful Movement, women must continue to give birth, past the point when it is medically safe, and if they die in childbirth, they are assured of their status in heaven as a martyr for God. Many Christian women are taught grounds for divorce might be abandonment or adultery but not abuse. The message this sends women is, "Suck it up, Sister" if you want to be a good wife in the eyes of the Church and patriarchy.

Boy children are valued while female babies are still killed at birth in poor countries because they may cost the family an expensive dowry later in life. We see in India and China there is a shortage of marriageable women because this practice of killing girl babies has been so prevalent. It is having a profound psychological effect on men, particularly poor men. Putting an actual face on this kind of atrocity, we learned at the Goddess Temple of Orange County the story of Fawzia Koofi, now called the Favored Daughter, but she was not always. She was left out in the sun to die by a mother who was ashamed of giving birth to a female in a society that honors only males, but miraculously, she lived and is now a member of the Afghani Parliament and will run for President of Afghanistan in the 2014 elections, if she survives.

Sexuality and our sacred blood is considered by some to be dirty and unclean and by association, so too are women, menstruation and female reproduction. Can you remember the public outcry when actress Demi Moore posed with her bare pregnant belly on a popular magazine? Even today women are cast out to the menstrual hut, but it was not always so. Once our sacred blood was seen as magical, a life-giving force coveted by men for its power.

Women today are still in danger of losing access to contraceptives and abortion in the United States, despite the latter being a constitutional right. Despite the recent election where the majority of Americans rejected their policies, Republican-controlled State Congresses continue their war on women passing laws restricting women's access to abortion and contraception. Some even require state-sanctioned internal vaginal probes against the order of doctors and require a woman to prove a miscarriage was not induced. Their legislation is forcing doctors to misinform their female patients, telling them if they have an abortion, they might never become pregnant again.

Women and attributes equated with the feminine consciousness are seen as inferior to men with far reaching consequences for both genders. We live in a country where "rugged individualism" is embraced by too many, with no consideration that the playing field is not level and where caring, sharing and nurturing, values of the Sacred Feminine, are considered weak or poverty is seen as a punishment from God, the authoritarian Father. Women are programmed to help perpetuate this list of sins rather than encouraging self-empowerment in a climate where women support women. Such men and their female handmaidens try to shame those of us calling for the empowerment and equality of women ugly words like Femi-Nazis, but we will not be silenced!

As we have forgotten the value in the belief of the intercon-

nectedness of all things, so too have we diminished and margin-
alized the important role of women as life-givers in the natural
order of the universe. Or when Republicans tout family values,
we quickly see it is more about abstinence, controlling women's
sexuality or forcing conformity via some religious dogma.

A sobering state of affairs for sure, but this is the herstory of
women on this planet. Let it be known so that we might cherry-
pick the best of our herstory and allow the light of transparency
to burn away the injustice. But this is surely not the end of the
story. Goddess is alive. She is being restored to the center of the
world, and we are here to write the next chapter of the story. We
are here writing a new mythology.

We are all dedicated to recovering the Great She, whether she
be deity, archetype or ideal. Yes, we intend to defy, to taste the
forbidden fruit, to be powerful and uppity women and men – not
patriarchal pawns or brainwashed sheeple. Every day we throw
off the shackles, look under every rock, behind every locked
door, peer into the abyss of the past so we know why things are
the way they are and shed light on the injustice! Why? So we can
explain how life has come to be turned on its head and become
so unnatural. And we're going to go about setting things right so
that we can save ourselves as a species and pull ourselves from
the brink. I think we have no other choice. If we want to restore
balance, harmony, wholeness, sanity, and equality, it is the We
and the Us, women and our like-minded brothers, armed with
ideas of the Sacred Feminine, who will set things back on course.

So now, I want to turn it over to you. Just as men once told of
the coming of the Judeo-Christian messiah, Jesus, it is your turn
to write the script and manifest the future. What does the coming
of the Messiah, She of Ten Thousand Names, bring to life on this
planet? How does rebirthing Goddess at the center of our hearts
and minds change society? Today. Here. Right now, let us vision
it so we might manifest it for ourselves. Stand up. Shout it out.
Let us hear your sacred roar! How do you see Goddess ideals

changing the world?

Note to speaker:

Encourage participation from the congregants. Ideas are listed below to "seed" the interaction.

End to violence against women. World peace. Our country's budget spent on uplifting the people and not the military industrial complex. Our tax dollars go to enhancing our quality of life, not corporate welfare. Political parties have women and children, the environment and life-affirming policies on their political platforms rather than the interests of corporations. Universal healthcare for all. Guaranteed education. Religious tolerance. Woman can be ordained as priests. Equal pay for equal work. Human rights for women across the globe. Greed is taboo and once again considered one of the Seven Deadly Sins. Anyone who commits violence against another human or animal is shamed by society. Rape of the earth is not tolerated. Natural resources are free for all people on the planet, and no longer can energy companies gouge us for what is rightfully ours. Likewise, no more wars over water. Environmentalism is part of our new religion. The inter-connectedness of all things is taught in our churches and schools. Women are not here to serve men. We see our bodies, our sacred blood, our sexuality, as sacred and divine once more. Everyone has the security of knowing they will earn a living wage and can retire in dignity. Empowering women is the moral imperative of our time. Women taking on the mantle of leadership, not waiting for it to be given to us. Red Tents and Women's Herstory are required learning for women and men across the globe!

Chapter 4

Balance in All Things

Today's message is about Balance in All Things. We could talk about the discipline to bring balance to your body and mind or in your personal life and in the context of the season, but instead, I want to talk about how our world being out of balance is a violation of Goddess ideals and suggest to you even an archetype like Kwan Yin is associated with justice, boundaries, and peace. I'd like to show how she is calling us to action to right the imbalances of the world if we go a bit deeper behind her sacred veil and examine some aspects of the Kwan Yin archetype, beneath the surface, hidden you might say, in plain sight! Goddess, you might say, becomes the great equalizer.

What comes to mind when you think of Kwan Yin, Mother of Compassion?

She is often associated with the Taoist Tien Hau, who has a temple in San Francisco, known for her caring, mercy, and for saving men lost at sea. She is closely associated with Isis, who also hears the prayers of her devotees, and Mary, the mother of Jesus, who is the intercessor between humans and God. Remember those apparitions of Our Lady known to appear in places like Lourdes, calling humanity to peace?

I think I felt the full potency of Kwan Yin energy when I was in Japan and met her counter-part, Kannon at the Sanju Sangendo Temple where there were 1001 statues of Kannon, each capable of 33 aspects, resulting in 33,033 manifestations of the Bodhisattva residing there.

I remember when I saw her for the first time. I didn't particularly relate to Kwan Yin or Kannon. I was there on a fact-finding mission researching my first book, *Sacred Places of Goddess: 108 Destinations*, and my appearance there was mostly business. To my surprise, Kannon got hold of me when I walked into the temple. The music, the incense, her energy just enveloped me. Now, I've been in many a temple, but there was something alive there. I was totally taken by surprise. I was captivated and in awe of her. I wanted to literally throw myself on the ground in front of her, but I felt silly and stopped myself because the room was filled with tourists. It was one of those moments you never forget, and it was one of those connections that makes you a believer she is alive out there!

So let's begin to see Kwan Yin in our mind's eye. She's an Asian Goddess, who wears flowing robes. She is usually tall and slender, sometimes nude or barefoot. Women turned to Kwan Yin when they were on the birthing bed or in their *struggle for freedom and recognition*. It was she who would bring their husbands back from war or the sea. It was believed she could understand their struggle, pain and suffering, and she lent them needed strength, love and compassion. She can be seen sitting on a lotus flower, fish, elephant or lion-like beast. Her image can also be one where she is nursing a baby or holding a child. Her symbols are a scroll of truth, a jar of healing water, and a spray of willow representing womanhood. She is often depicted with her feet on a dragon.

The numbers vary widely, so let's just say she has 33 manifestations and 11 heads enabling her to hear and see the cries of the needy and to answer their prayers. She also has 1,000 hands in which she holds a vase containing amitra, or the dew of compassion, which she pours forth upon humankind to extend life, cure, and purify the body, mind and speech. Kannon held objects too, to fight off all manner of misfortune that might befall humanity: a rosary, trident, sword, lotus, bow and arrows, ax, mirror, wheel, and bell. I couldn't help but think of the female warrioresses in the movie, *Crouching Tiger, Hidden Dragon*.

I think when patriarchy allows us to glimpse the Sacred Feminine, it wants us to see a very narrow and limiting picture of Goddess me might feel we must emulate in order to serve man or patriarchy's authoritarian god. She is demure and mutable, a woman out of balance and not in touch with her power. Sure, they approve of the nubile sex goddess here for man's pleasure or the giving mother without personal boundaries to protect herself, the healer wiping the nose of the sick child or the tears from suffering eyes, or the crone who dedicates her time to keeping the church altar clean. We're allowed to have the Great Mother in our spiritual paradigm if she is docile and tame like Mary, or as the Goddess that saves women in childbirth or men from bombs and typhoons. But would patriarchy have us reclaim the full meaning of the Queen Mother of Compassion, or any Goddess, if it meant embodying her might bring our world into balance and emulating her caused women to no longer serve the status quo? If we saw beyond the dew of compassion and the rosary and evaluated what else is hidden in plain sight? If we looked at her ax, bow and arrows, sword, and trident as tools or metaphors of resistance? If we interpreted why she holds the bell, or has her feet on a dragon or has as one of her symbols, the scroll of truth? I think looking more deeply at goddesses like Kwan Yin/Kannon might make the patriarchy very nervous.

Kwan Yin energy is not merely that of an obedient consort or spouse, a healer, servant or helper of god and man. She is no Stepford Wife, passive, sexless, docile, tame and complicit in her own oppression.

No, she is armed, literally and metaphorically. She is also fierce compassion with the power to protect, defend, be activated and motivated. She holds truth important – a thing more valuable than gold. Truth, something many would keep from you because in truth there is wisdom, knowledge and power. In the light of truth, darkness, injustice and oppression cannot thrive.

The ringing of her chimes cuts through the din of chaos bringing forth clarity for critical thinking so you might not be held hostage, duped and led astray.

And what of her weapons – the bow and arrows, trident, ax, and sword? Well, Goddesses have long held weapons and instruments of change and activation. Isis' sistrum kept the energies of the universe flowing. What of Mary's role of intercessor, one who actively intercedes? Does this not clearly tell us we must be ready, willing and able to stand up and wage peace? We must be warrioresses and activists for her ideals: fairness, justice, equality and partnership. No more than we can find a job by just praying and thinking positive thoughts can we be serious about changing the world without being activated and motivated. Just as we must send out resumes and network for a job, we must rally and ally with the like-minded if want to change the world. We must gather all our resources both on the magical and mundane spheres to empower ourselves and manifest the world we vision. Use Kwan Yin's sword to cut through the doubt until you find certainty. Shifts do happen. Remember, once Christians met in living rooms, and look at the influence they have become on Mother Earth. Shifts, dreams, and visions become realities with proper action, intention, support, focus and fierce compassion.

As we are called to be a way-shower, foremother, defender, healer, or warrioress, what is *our* ax, bow and arrows, trident and sword? How do we go forward in the world blazing a trail with our pink-handled machete? What are our weapons?

I say to you our weapons are many, and we need them all because patriarchy will not just roll over and die because we will it, pray for it or think positive thoughts.

Our books of knowledge are our weapons, because knowledge is power. Has not patriarchy tried their best to keep knowledge of Goddess and women's natural leadership and spiritual authority from us?

Intuition is our weapon. Women intuitively know how to birth life, nurture and multi-task. They are the glue keeping homes, businesses, and organizations going. If women stopped serving the status quo, if they stopped volunteering tomorrow, how many would collapse?

Our voice is our weapon. Has patriarchy not tried to make us content and satisfied being subservient and our power diminished? We must all find our "sacred rage and our sacred roar" and let our wisdom and intellect reverberate out across the ethers to be heard by all.

Our written word is our weapon, for the pen can be mightier than the sword. Each of you sitting here has changed her life not at the point of a dagger but because of the information you have no doubt read or been taught.

Our tenacity and strength are our weapons. Any woman who has birthed or raised a child, had a book published, started an organization, manifested a temple – they all know the strength, courage and determination women possess. Remember women, we do 80% of the work around the world even if, under patriarchy, we only earn 20% of the assets!

Our weapons are our innate ability to intuit, to love and nurture, to support our sisters, to tend and befriend in times of stress. We must begin to stand shoulder to shoulder, **thinking of the Us and We, not the I and Me.**

Our weapon is the wisdom we embody and the power of the life-affirming Creatrix, while patriarchy is the obsolete and forceful destroyer. We must remember who we are!

This is just a short list, and I'm sure you can no doubt think of many more weapons in our female toolkit or arsenal.

The Dalai Lama said it would be Western Women who would save the world. He's close to being right. It will be humankind shifting toward the ideals of the Sacred Feminine and eco-feminist spirituality that will save the world. It will be women and our like-minded brothers finding their sacred roar, uncovering forbidden knowledge, living, writing and teaching their wisdom and truth, standing in their power as leaders, and fighting for their values. All that will shift consciousness. It must be all that, coming together like a delicious stew which will make it so.

All this sounds fine and good in theory, doesn't it? But how does recognizing Kwan Yin or Kannon as a tenacious, kick-ass warrior Goddess armed with not just compassion but her weaponry help us today? How is it relevant? How do we apply it? Well, let me help you connect the dots.

First, like Kwan Yin, our community is multi-armed and has many heads, eyes, and hands. We must be multi-taskers because the dominance and force of patriarchy has left us with much to correct. There are many vital causes that need attention. There is not just one task that needs correction, and fortunately, many of us are called to serve on different paths.

You might feel called to:

Teach classes and write books.
Be an environmental or animal rights activist.
Use your sacred roar via some form of media.
Raise Goddess-aware children or grandchildren.
Work as a healer or in hospice care.
Become a sacred bee priestess.
Inform and shift consciousness through your art.
Promote healthy living and eating.
Public service as a priestess or politician.

At the very least, you're seeing how all the ways our world is out of balance are direct challenges or violations of Goddess ideals or earth-based spirituality. Yes, we must choose between darkness and light, good and evil, oppression and liberation, equality and injustice. We must have balance between environmentalism and deregulation, rugged individualism versus caring and sharing, left versus right brain thinking, activism versus apathy. What about the imbalance of income and opportunity between the Haves and the Have Nots?

Yes, Gaia as Mother Nature teaches us how very important

balance is and the cost of imbalance, and I think when we see her weapons, she is telling us we must fight for that which we hold dear and what we know is right.

Friends, we are being called to change the world from the inside out. We aren't talking about tinkering around the edges if we want a society that makes decisions based on truth, one that's really fair and balanced, that's just and whole and values and practices equality and peace. If we want to embody Goddess, we aren't just the power behind the throne; WE ARE THE THRONE! Remember, it was Isis who granted the pharaoh the right to rule, and she expected him to do so employing the aspects of the Goddess Ma'at, namely justice and truth, and dare I say, fierce compassion, too!

Isis isn't our only role model. Neither is Mary as intercessor, or Our Lady appearing and advising us to wage peace. There is a beautiful tapestry of herstory out there with many women, and each is a colorful thread making a difference not just in their own realms but worldwide: Boudica, Joan of Arc, Cleopatra, Women in the Bible, Hildegard von Bingen, Mother Theresa, Lady Di, sibyls and oracles, midwives, women and priestesses of contemporary and ancient times who held life and death in their hands. Consider today's Catholic Nuns on the Bus making their nationwide bus tour teaching about the immorality of extremist Republican budgets and ideology, women who fought for their rights to control their bodies and fates, women who suffered for our right to vote, for civil rights, and for worker rights, and women who fought the patriarchy of the Church, who were burned at the stake or who died for our democracy. We might not always know their names because history was written by the conquering, rich, patriarchs, all too often leaving the names of women out of the history books.

Every time we are called to the voting booth, will we let the rich patriarchs have their way again? Will we let angry, white, privileged, conservative billionaire men who are distorting our media, buying our democracy, stacking the deck of the Supreme Court for the benefit of the banks, the corporations and the 1%, who threaten our rights and our futures, will we let them win? Or will enough women and their like-minded brothers find their sacred rage and rise up with their sword and the fierce compassion of Kwan Yin, beating back the dragon so we might have more balance in our world?

Goddess doesn't roll over in the face of adversity, and neither should we. Remember the weapons in the hands of Kwan Yin. Remember Kali, Sekhmet, the Morrighan, Nemesis, Artemis, Libertas, Metis and Isis. We have an obligation to fight for social justice, to set healthy boundaries, to help the world find balance and not be willing victims of patriarchal oppression.When it's time to make a choice, find your sacred rage and your sacred roar. Volunteer, vote and be a civic minded advocate for truth, sanity, fairness, equality and social justice. Don't moan that you didn't get everything you wanted. Don't be drawn into the false equivalence that today's Democrats and Republicans are all the same. They are not! Democrats aren't legislating forced vaginal probes be inserted in your vagina against your will!

Then, when the election is over, sit down and have a hard look at yourself. If you haven't already, rediscover your own passion or calling. How are you going to help change the world? As I've said, I'm not talking about tinkering around the edges. What can or must you do to help bring the world into balance? What do you feel so strongly about that you would arm yourself with both your own waters of compassion, as well as your sword, trident and quiver of arrows like our Compassionate Warrior Queen, Kwan Yin? What will you tame as Kwan Yin does as she sits upon her lion or puts her foot upon the head of a dragon?

Note to reader: In non-election cycles, you might omit references to voting and elections.

Chapter 5

Our Real Wealth

Let's talk a little about our bounty, our riches, and our good fortune.

We all play the lottery, probably. I know I do. We think if we just made more money or had some kind of windfall, it would make our lives better. We even say when we do prosperity rituals, "Let the riches comes from whatever source the universe might provide, as long as it harms none, and it's best for all concerned." But let's look at this a bit closer.

What are our *real* riches, bounty, and good fortune – the operative word being *real*? Where do the *real* riches come from? What's the source?

I recently learned that Lakshmi, Hindu Goddess of bounty in all things, is often seen on Indian banks, and some Hindu families will refer to their wife or daughter as their Lakshmi. In other words, the women in their families embody their good fortune. Sometimes families without girl children will invite female relatives to live with them to bring the bounty of Lakshmi into their lives.

What about knowledge? Certainly that's our bounty, especially knowledge that comes from herstory or Goddess Spirituality.

For instance, we learn in male-dominated society we define power as *power over* others and the desire to control. But we learn in Women's Studies, within Goddess Spirituality, that's not a healthy definition of power. In fact, we might discuss if *power over* something is bounty at all. What a double-edged sword that is. Real bounty comes not from having *power over*, but the confidence *in oneself* and real power *for oneself*. This reduces the need to have *power over* others or to control them. We don't have to diminish others to assert our own strength. What a bounty it is to know the distinction of this important concept and work toward creating a society using that ideal!

We know that many goddess temples of the ancient world were centers of financial power and were presided over by priestesses, even though today most of the financial institutions of our society are still presided over by men. It's important to know women once wielded the bounty of the people. Barbara Walker teaches that silver and gold coins were valuable not because they were made of precious metals that came from the earth, from the body of Gaia, but because the coins were believed to be blessings from Goddess herself ,which were believed to bring good fortune and healing magic, making money a magical invention! Let's consider the Goddess, Juno Moneta. It's interesting that Moneta means **She Who Gives Warning**. That's a perfect segue for the rest of what I want to share with you.

Coming back to the lottery, some of you may have heard anecdotal evidence for lottery winners being cursed. I know within Kabbalah teachings they believe that because they say something not earned cannot bring you long-term good fortune. I'm not saying life isn't easier with money, but again, money is a double-edged sword. When you have a lot of it, you have to wonder if your friends and family love you or your money. Look at the care you have to take to keep it and grow it and not be robbed. Someone I've known a long time has been a good teacher for me on this subject. The man is rich. His father is richer and has a huge house in Beverly Hills, CA with more solar panels on it than the apartment complex where I live. My friend is so busy running the family business, keeping the money flowing in, he has no life. I pity him because he rarely seems happy. I would describe him as trapped by his wealth.

You might say, well, that's just what people who don't have a lot of money say. They marginalize money. Well, I think it's about balance. I think we need *enough* money, but we need to know when enough is enough; otherwise it turns into greed. Kabbalah studies can be very interesting. In their teachings you learn you should desire more and more, but not for yourself. The abundance is really to make the lives of others better. In fact, *giving is your security*. Giving and sharing is your ticket to being safe in a dangerous world. Your blessings, your bounty, comes to you when you give to others; in fact, they think if you give until it hurts – of your time, your care, the benefit of your skills – you get even more bounty or good fortune.

So let's think about bounty beyond money. What floats your boat? What makes you feel rich, happy and fulfilled?

Personally, I've come to know for myself, *things* do not make me happy, nor do they help me feel fulfilled. I'll confide that I was married to my high school sweetheart. Early on, in my twenties, I already had a house and two cars and as much money as I needed, and my husband was a nice guy, but that was not my bounty. I was not happy or fulfilled. I was yearning, seeking, empty and unfulfilled. There was a hole in me I filled with doing ceramics and raising spider plants, all sorts of things to keep me busy. I don't even think I was consciously aware of the hole in me. I know I just never felt fulfilled. I had what everyone strives for, didn't I? I had what everyone says is what we should want out of life.

Fast forward. Life is very different now. My husband, Roy, and I have been married almost 30 years. Having the right partner in my life has been the foundation for my bounty. I could make more money working in corporate America, but I don't. I've traded making more money for quality of life. Finding Goddess and sharing those ideals, being in service to the Great She, to the community, is probably the most nourishing thing I do, next to learning and being with those I love and having women who challenge my thinking and ideas. This is my purpose. I think getting older, having experience, and acquiring some wisdom has also contributed to my riches and good fortune because I have liberated myself from worrying so much about what people say and think about me, and I no longer feel I have to be perfect in everything I do. I just have to do my best. When my cats come up and sit next to me, with one on each arm of my chair, they make me feel like I'm Cybele sitting on my throne; or when someone emails me thanking me for doing my radio show because it's their lifeline, these are the kinds of things that help me know I'm rich.

So these are some examples of what I'd say are my riches. What are yours? What is your purpose? That's important to think about because how often do you hear about someone retiring from their job, and they drop dead because they have nothing to live for. Their purpose has ended. Or they win the lottery and they get arrogant, stop caring, drop out, stop relating, and don't make wise investments in their life – and I'm not just talking about money. They become an empty vessel. How many people think gold, diamonds, drugs, alcohol, power, or food will fill that gaping hole inside of them? Does the latest computer or gadget fulfill you? What about designer shoes or clothes? A new car every year? Do they fulfill you? But for how long? Is it real fulfillment? Or is it fool's gold? Does that brief glimpse of happiness fade?

What fills your vessel to overflowing? Is it good friends? Supportive family? Great conversation? Travel? Making discoveries? Going to the ocean and feeling at one with the ebb and flow of the Mother? Laying in the grass looking up at the sky? Maybe it's music or learning? Being appreciated or helping others? Debating a concept? Your lover's warm embrace? Cool sheets on a Spring morning? Satisfaction from a goal satisfied?

What feeds you? That's your real riches and bounty. That's what will bring you good fortune. Remember Joseph Campbell said, *"Follow your bliss."* Follow your bliss and riches will flow.

Most importantly, when you find what feeds you, Goddess teaches you to nurture and tend to those things, just like you tend a garden. Tend to your friendships. Nurture the things that fulfill you. Whatever it is that makes you feel rich, don't neglect it. If you're finding yourself feeling empty, at a loss, or poor, then maybe you haven't been tending your life's garden. As I remind listeners on my radio show, Mother Nature, Gaia herself teaches us, what we tend to and nurture thrives. What we neglect withers, and we're left with nothing, and that's real poverty. So, to conclude, we are probably all rich. We just have to focus on defining what our bounty and riches are and the source of our good fortune.

Chapter 6

Fires of Transformation

Have you given fire much thought lately? I mean have you *really* thought about fire – particularly as an instrument of change and transformation? You might have realized the four elements are not just components of the universe, or Gaia, but of our own inner psyches or temperament as well. Earth is more than synonymous with the cardinal direction of the north and the physical land upon which we walk, but it embodies who we are, and the gateway to manifestation. It is our physical journey of life. Water is not only representative of the westerly direction, it is also our emotions, inner vision, feelings and intuition. Air, in the east, represents our psyche's ability to know, communicate, clarify, and contemplate. Air fuels the vehicles of our creations.

Fire, creative and destructive, and perhaps the most potentially volatile of the elements, hails from the south. It is the heat that stokes our passion and sexuality and arouses our will. It is the catalyst for growth and transformation. Experiencing the fire within, we are transmuted, and we affect factors outside ourselves, like falling dominoes, triggering, sparking, activating, and inciting further change. With fire we take flight, we purify, we morph, we explode onto the world and transition from one thing to another. Unlike the other elements, fire does not exist in a natural state. It takes physical form by overtaking or consuming the other elements, thus it is the master transformer. It is affected by the other three substances and vice versa.

Alone, fire, or the sun, creates heat or temperature, but add air, and the planet has weather. Add wind to a small flame, and you might create a firestorm. Add fire to oxygen, and you have an explosion. When certain elements of the earth mix with flame, we create bronze, iron or copper instruments, weaponry or jewelry. Lasers come to mind as coming from a form of fire, as well as electricity or solar power. Add the rays of the sun to growing things and photosynthesis occurs. With too much heat and not enough water, dehydration and withering occurs. Add water to fire, and we get steam or combustion. Scientists say the ultimate fiery explosion, the Big Bang, spewed forth the planets of the universe. Add the warmth of heat to food, and we have cooking. Mix fire with potions, and we have created medicine. Ancient alchemists were believed to be able to apply fire to base metals to create gold. Anyone who has sat around a campfire or by a crackling hearth knows the trance-like state the dancing flames might induce. Even the destructive nature of wild fire or lava is known to have positive benefits of purifying and cleansing, making way for new growth.

Fire's active and projective nature gives us the strength, endurance, passion and will to grow and change. It enables us to stand in our truth and integrity and face adversity. Fire can be synonymous with the growing pains of coming into one's own power. It is about fashioning the tools of trust, faith and prayer to help us in times of need. It about standing firm when our abilities and beliefs are tested. It is about maneuvering the treacherous gauntlet of politics. Fire helps us burn away fear and self-doubt. We emerge from the cauldron steeled, liberated and empowered. We have all heard of trials by fire. Life sometimes throws those tests our way, and how we respond is the measure of who we are. Fire demands we stand up and be counted and help lead the way.

How we manage our fire may take the form of how we maneuver in the world within personal relationships, business or social partnerships and spiritual communities. Can we manage volatile situations tempering hostility and fear with diplomacy and reason? How do we manage our will and passion? Our ego and ambition? Are they in harmony and balance? Are they responsibly and compassionately directed? Are we a steady flame, or do we burn out quickly? In other words, are we tenacious and focused to get a job done, or do we tend to give up and not have staying power? Fire teaches us about anger, rage and boundaries. For a long time, women were taught to be nice, not make waves, and be charming and polite. These can all be positive attributes under the right circumstances. Fire teaches one to know her personal boundaries and learn to say no without guilt when someone crosses a line. Fire gives one permission to have justifiable anger and rage. Fire enables us to dare and risk, but we must be sure we temper that with reason.

Fire is about tapping into and harnessing the energy of the universe as well as the personal power or potential within. It is about learning to direct that power toward an intention for positive effect or healing. This can be called prayer or magic. Having good motivations and intention is of utmost importance when projecting one's will. Fire is also about knowing when to surrender and trust.

Obviously fire is about change and transformation. It can be an obvious positive change or an uncomfortable transition, but often I have found even the latter was not without benefit; you just have to look for the gift. Can you see the benefit a wild fire or spewing lava might bring? Fire gives us the tenacity to break bad habits and perhaps cleanse ourselves of dis-ease. We can further work with fire as a symbol for authority, leadership and self-empowerment. This can be done using visualization or with direction of our will in prayer and meditations, alone or in group ritual. More linear methods, such as research and study, might be employed as well, especially when you have to tenaciously dig deep and find the facts.

Goddess Spirituality provides a toolbox of practices to help us understand fire, harness it and make the powerful element our friend. We can use archetypes of fire and work with the aspects associated with that power using sacred symbols or individual Goddesses such as the lion-headed, Egyptian Goddess, Sekhmet.

The Lady of Tenacity Manifested, is the new name I have coined for Sekhmet, adding to her thousands of ancient ones. After walking with her for years, discussing her with Rev. Patricia Pearlman, former caretaker of the Sekhmet Temple outside Las Vegas, Nevada, I believe Sekhmet teaches courage, strength and integrity. Those who fear Sekhmet fear their own power. For women she is particularly important because she teaches us to empower ourselves, to know our strength, and to never let another take our power away. She schools us in confidence and sends lessons our way to steel and enable us. She allows us to grow and find the inner drive and determination to see things through. She is that energy and power down deep inside that can be called up when we must stand up and be counted, to speak out, or to make things happen. She teaches us to say no. As such, she is the perfect Goddess for male and female feminists who are tenaciously struggling for a world of justice and equality. Her lesson of tenacity is not unlike water that wears away rock, bit by bit, slowly, continually, never giving up. She is the constant ebb and flow, back and forth, one step forward, two steps back, until success is achieved.

Sekhmet is associated with the sun, which can either be life giving and sustaining or deadly under adverse or careless circumstances. In understanding this aspect she teaches us diligence and discernment. As we come into our power, we must also come to know the importance of employing care, personal responsibility and accountability in all we do.

Genevieve Vaughan, benefactress of the Sekhmet Temple outside Las Vegas, draws comparisons between the legend of Sekhmet, in which she went on a rampage caused by the evil of people, to an appropriate warning for us now because we allow ourselves to be drugged into giving up the political and economic power that we could use to stop the destruction of the Earth. She said we should heed Sekhmet's warnings and stop sipping the drug of lies allowing ourselves to be disemboweled by consumerism and substance abuse. She sees Sekhmet as a liberated human animal who will not allow the destruction of Mother Earth. Sekhmet has become an icon and archetype of immanent Female Power.

In this Goddess, this archetype of fire and transformation, we see all phases of women. She is the lioness mother, regal, independent, instructive, loyal, and playful as she indulges her cubs; yet she is certainly capable of destruction if she must protect herself or her children. She is might and right, and one feels safe in her embrace. She works in partnership beside other lionesses in her pride to feed and protect her family; or she goes it alone when necessary, standing in her own authority and authenticity. A mother and healer, it is said she created humanity with either her tears or breath. Her consort, Ptah, is the Egyptian builder God and her son, Mehes, the patron of doctors. She is the stuff of creation, not devastation as a patriarchal myth would have you believe. Beautiful and capable, the essence of transformation, you call upon her to assist you to remove obstacles with her power and blinding light. See her golden eyes as lasers able to crumble the most formidable foes. In rituals she may be called upon to heal us physically and mentally, and we might enlist her strength to help us banish what no longer serves us. To embody Sekhmet, to feel her fire, is to become the empowered woman or man capable of standing up to life's challenges and accomplishing your goals. To know her is to be able to find your sacred roar to change yourself and the world.

Chapter 7

The Liberation of Surrender

What images come to mind when you hear the word *surrender*? For me I doubt I thought much about it beyond seeing an old television show where one side raises the white flag because they've been defeated. Surrender was not a concept I thought much about. Neither was my need for control.

Instead, like so many others in denial about their illusion of control or with a penchant for perfectionism, I believed I staved off chaos with organization, attention to detail and lists. These tools help, of course, and lists made me feel safe. I have daily lists, weekly lists, monthly and annual lists. Nothing makes me feel better than an entire list with big fat red lines through all the things that have been completed. And throwing a list away, with everything finally complete, well now, that's almost orgasmic! But sometimes the best planning does not guarantee an outcome matches our perception of perfection or success. It took a metaphoric two-by-four bopping me between the eyes a few times before I caught on. Let me explain.

Thoughts of surrender were the farthest thing from my mind as I departed for Ireland to be ordained as clergy and to meet Lady Olivia Robertson, one of the founders of the International Fellowship of Isis at Clonegal Castle. Before leaving home, I'd meticulously taken care of all the preparations, not just for my sacred journey, but for a group pilgrimage I was arranging for others traveling to Egypt in a few months. Months and months of hard work went into that pilgrimage. Imagine the number of lists that involved! But while in Ireland, I heard the BBC telecast about the tourists in Egypt that had been gunned down. I knew cancellations would begin to flood in.

Demoralized and disappointed, I sat at the breakfast table of my B&B just outside Clonegal Castle, head in hands, and I'm not ashamed to admit I cried. How could so much hard work and such good intentions, helping people make a sacred journey, be threatened in such a way – not just for me but for those pilgrims? Then, like a fairy from the emerald meadows outside my window, Bridie, the proprietress, sat down next to me and began to talk. In a soothing voice, she gently talked and talked. She shared how business had been bad this year for her family and things looked really bleak. She revealed she was really scared and heartbroken, but she had faith things were going to turn around. She told me she just kept trying and wouldn't give up. Bridie's generosity of spirit, compassion and kindness touched me on many levels, and my angst began to diminish. Before too long I gathered myself, made some calls to the State to keep the threads from unraveling on my group going to Egypt and went on to Clonegal Castle for my ordination ceremony. I will remember that day as long as I live. To think, in my angst, I almost did not go.

By the time I returned home from Ireland, things had settled down in Egypt and in the media. The group of pilgrims I sent to Egypt was very different than I originally visioned, but they had a memorable journey. Disaster averted, I soon forgot about Bridie's wise words in Ireland.

Time passed and as one might expect, life continued to deal out all sorts of challenges. Disillusionment and disappointment threatened to drive me from this path of Goddess Spirituality altogether. Under a rock or the shadows seemed a much more comfortable place to be, but just as Bridie had appeared during dark times in Ireland, help came in the guise of the lion-headed Egyptian Goddess, Sekhmet, whose essence and archetype brought lessons for passion, tenacity and strength.

Not right away, but in time, I began to realize the obstacles being presented to me were in fact important detours and guide-posts, forcing me down new paths I might not have imagined were my life's journey. People who made me crazy were simply pawns of the Universe providing the opportunity for lessons that needed to be learned in this life. Still with all life's distractions, with the struggle and angst averted, when we are feeling happy and fulfilled, we sometimes forget those lessons that things are often really beyond our control, that we cannot always see the good reasons behind pain and frustration, and that outcomes are often not in our hands. We learn that wisdom teaches us we are measured by how we respond to the challenges we face. How do we treat people? Do we appreciate what we have? Are we grateful for those that make our lives easier and happier? Do we see the glass as half full? Are we reactive or proactive?

Fast forward. I received an email out of the blue. My publisher was gifting me with six-hundred fifty pounds of new books which needed to be accepted, signed for, unloaded and stored. So what did I do? I began making my lists, of course! I made arrangements for labor to move the 22 cases of books and for UPS to deliver on a certain day. I even discovered the shipping labels on all 22 cases were wrong and fortunately caught the mistake before a misdelivery. Surely now all I needed to do was clear some storage space and sit back and wait for the shipment. But guess what? Despite all the careful planning, I came home from a weekend trip to find those 22 cases of books had been delivered two days early and had been sitting unsecured in the hallway of my apartment building. But alas, it was all good. Not a case was tampered with. Phew! Relief. But it wasn't over.

I took a deep breath and tore into the closest case to look at a long awaited copy of this new book, *Walking an Ancient Path, Rebirthing Goddess on Planet Earth*. Within a few minutes I felt that all too familiar snake-like creep of panic and anxiety inching up my spine. Not only were there *blank pages* in the new book, but after all the extra time double checking, triple checking, list making, and email exchanges with the publisher, the final edits didn't make it into this printing. Damn! Imagine the embarrassment and frustration!

But then, much more quickly than ever before, not in days or months, but within minutes, the upset began to dissipate and *remembering* kicked in. It was as if a light came on in my mind. The lessons of Ireland and Bridie, of Sekhmet's lessons of tenacity, of the book delivery, of other times of dark clouds with silver linings, it all came rushing back to me in a wave, and I actually began to laugh out loud. Like a lightning bolt, I heard a voice in my head:

> *You cannot control everything. You can only do the best that you can do; then you have to surrender to what is to come. Have you not learned this lesson yet, Karen? Have you not truly benefited from life's curve balls? You must put away fear of criticism, fear of failure, fear of imperfection. I don't ask that you be the smartest or the best. I only ask that you **do your best** and allow this faith to make you fearless.*

So what did I do? What any woman does, of course! I called one of my sisters about the revelation. I started telling Lora about Bridie in Ireland, Sekhmet, the 22 cases of books and about the botched printing of what turned out to be just a few copies of that book! We laughed together at this concept of learning the liberation of surrender! I realized it's learning to trust in the wisdom of the Universe, or Goddess. Then Lora shared the email from her Messenger's Circle that arrived that very morning:

> *On this day of your life, dear friend, I believe God/ess wants you to know....that perfectionism is the enemy of creation. Nothing stops the forward march of any creative endeavor like the need to do it absolutely perfectly. And who is to judge what is "perfect" anyway? What I have judged full of flaws so many others have called*

terrific. Maybe the definition of perfection is something that actually gets done.

It felt like another validating voice from heaven, and laughingly, we swore to make *perfectionism is the enemy of creation* our mantra and tape it to our computer desks. We actually contemplated bumper stickers!

But in hindsight, I feel what was also important besides our personal epiphanies was that I had to lay my soul bare, risk my soft underbelly and share this with everyone, because we all have so much we can do, and there is so little time. So many of us have much we want to share, no matter our calling, but something hinders us and holds us back. Doubt breeds procrastination or inaction. We are afraid of not doing it perfectly or that others can do it better, or we are waiting for someone else to step up.

I'm suggesting you must be fearless and *just do it!* Not one of us can afford to hide our light under a bushel because of the fear of success or failure. We cannot be paralyzed by things that may happen beyond our control or fear our imperfections or the criticism people might lay at our doorstep. Just know that they will criticize, and follow your passion or inner voice anyway. We just must do our best. We must strive to liberate ourselves and surrender to the certainty we are playing our part in this macrocosm. We must honor and trust in the wisdom of the Universe to provide exactly what it is we need. We must remember we are each powerful players in the dance of creation, and in these moments of angst, there is a gift; we just have to look for it.

So, I am sharing my hard learned lesson with all of you. Learn to be proactive and look for the gifts in life's challenges. See Goddess when she shines her light down a different path. Appreciate life and don't let fear create your reality. Just go out into the world and be the best you can be. Go out into the world *and do!*

Chapter 8

Harmony from Chaos

We would be remiss to not state the obvious. Judeo-Christian patriarchal culture teaches man is entitled to be the master of Nature, and by association, the female gender. Mankind reveled in his feelings of entitlement given to him by his sky god. He possessed it all and used it as he saw fit, with a green light from his religion. So society forgot, or perhaps never learned, our obligation not to exploit. Too many of us forgot our obligation to be wise stewards of Nature, working in harmony with all else in our giant web, this macrocosm, which we all share together. Humankind forgot our obligation to be in balance and harmony with all living things, including the female gender. We became disconnected from each other and the energy of the Universe. We were broken and fragmented. We certainly became disconnected from the ideals of the Mother. All was in disharmony.

This was not always the norm. The Ancients understood the delicate balance, this dance between the masculine and feminine energies. One wonders if Kabbalah teachings, which predate the Bible, might have been influenced by matriarchies when we learn they teach that a man must embrace the Sacred Feminine within himself to lead a rich and fulfilled life. We once knew there must be harmony, a partnership if you will, between the energies of masculine and feminine.

Indigenous peoples living close to the land understood the importance of living in harmony with Nature. Native Americans honored Mother Earth equally with Father Sky, and it was their belief not to take more from the earth than they needed to sustain themselves. Aboriginal peoples are so closely connected to the land that men and women speak of feeling in their very bones any abuse heaped upon their sacred lands. The myths of the Inuit

Goddess, Sedna, reflect ready-made environmental balances to keep the natural world safe from overuse and exploitation. We can see in Egyptian wall reliefs the Goddess Isis handing the pharaoh Ma'at, or the right to rule the people. Yes, he received that authority from She of 10,000 Names. But what was Ma'at?

Embodied in the personification of the great Goddess, Ma'at, that winged Goddess with the feather on her head, was the ancient Egyptian understanding of this principle of balance and harmony. Her name literally meant "truth" in Egyptian. She was truth, order, balance and justice in the guise of the Sacred Feminine. She was harmony. She was what was right. She was how things should be. It was the responsibility of the pharaoh to rule his people utilizing the principles of Ma'at. It was thought that if Ma'at didn't exit, the universe would become chaos once again.

Does it not feel sometimes as if that is exactly what we have today? Turn on the news, and the world is certainly in chaos. We hear about Abrahamic fundamentalism turning into terrorism and the resulting loss of life. We see economic terrorism, and many of us feel the direct effects of disaster or predator capitalism. We see the disharmony from the imbalance of power in the United States, whether it be within political parties, or as corporations battling workers, or as the rich taking more and more of the pieces of the pie, all creating chaos and disharmony in the lives of The Many. We see conservative Right-Wing fundamentalist ideology taking constitutional rights away from women, trying to deny gays the rights to marry, even causing young gay men and lesbians to commit suicide because they are told they are an abomination in the eyes of the Abrahamic God. We've been waging war in foreign countries across the globe for more than a decade, yet we rarely hear about the human casualties, the loss of life, the families split apart, the maimed, the real number of dead, or the women forced into prostitution and human trafficking. All that collateral damage. All that chaos and disharmony. Pain and atrocities may be swept under the rug and sanitized but are nevertheless real.

Of course there is chaos beyond our control, such as some natural disasters, but juxtapose that with the chaos chosen or imposed on others by the powerful, like corporations destroying natural resources, the debt ceiling faux-emergency or the sequester – all that drama and suffering that disproportionately affects the powerless and poor, the middle class and most needy. What about the long lines people had to stand in to vote? Does this not all feel like a form of manipulation created by certain factions who feel entitled to wreak havoc, to act irresponsibly or selfishly rather than to seek harmony and what is best for all the citizenry?

But let's again think about the nature of disharmony and chaos, both multilayered and complicated in their design. Can either actually be a good thing sometimes? Can real change, new life, and new beginnings actually come from chaos? What about the Big Bang? Think about the labors of childbirth, the messy, chaotic and painful process, yet what comes forth is the promise of new life. Think about the social justice movements across the globe as people fight for their rights, protest against austerity and seek out a more hopeful future. Wildfires and lava flows actually benefit the soil in the long view.

Think about the chaos in communities or within relationships. Can anyone here remember the confusing and chaotic feelings of love? Divorce? Political chaos? Remember the chaos in Wisconsin that woke up the middle class and got them on their feet? We watched the Egyptian Spring as the oppressed from all walks of life stood together, risking their very lives, in what seemed like sheer chaos at times, to bring the hope of opportunity and freedom into their lives. Chaos and disharmony is unsettling, ugly or disorienting, but it's like stirring the cauldron. It's like rattling the sistrum. We shake up the energies of the universe to keep things from being stagnant. So perhaps we can see that sometimes chaos is a necessary thing, a catalyst toward change – even paradigm shifts. Chaos can lead to good things, so let us not fear chaos, but let us try to grab the hope, the potent ideas or the building blocks from that chaos so that good may be the outcome.

Let's face it; when it comes to eco-feminism or Goddess, did we think we would rebirth Sacred Feminine ideals in our times in absolute harmony? Did we think that authoritarian Father would vanish because we willed it or prayed for it? Did we think the patriarchal power of rich capitalists and organized religion would roll over and play dead, or give up power and control easily? Does anyone who has their tentacles in us give us up easily? No, that extrication is painful. They create chaos and wedge issues to divide us. Sometimes it's a tactic, stirring fear, encouraging confusion with disinformation. In their attempt to retain their power over us, their game is to divide and conquer; propaganda, culture wars, racial tension, pitting gay against straight, immigrants against citizens, conservatives against liberals, union workers against non-union workers, and low information voters against themselves take our eyes off the real enemies of harmony, peace, sustainability and balance.

I know I've heard more times than I care to that the problem is the teachers, the firefighters, the unions that protect the workers, or the poor, all those takers, sometimes referred to as the 47% by former presidential hopeful, Mitt Romney, or the 99%. They are the enemy, we're told, so no light may shine on the real creators of the chaos, which would upset the apple cart of the status quo. Conservatives are known to support the institutions simply for the sake of stability, even though there are those at the bottom of our dominator society suffering greatly for that illusion of security and sustainability. So when we strive for harmony, let us not be blind to the benefits of shaking things up, of chaos.

Some of this chaos and disharmony we as individuals cannot

do a lot about. Yes, we can vote, sign petitions, march in the street, boycott companies that abuse the environment and their workers, write our politicians, maybe even run for office ourselves. We the People can join groups that give us the numbers to fight Big Money, but in our everyday lives, 24/7, what can we do to increase harmony in the short term, in our personal lives and in our families and communities?

Well, we can start by getting toxic people out of our lives. We can know the issues so we don't accidentally support people working against our interests. We can try to communicate better and not be reactionary. Cut out the drama. Everyone remember Mr. Spock on *Star Trek*? Did you ever envy his cool? We can restrict ourselves and strive for moderation. We can negotiate and practice partnership instead of having to have it all one way, or our way. We can value diversity. We can put the shoe on the other foot and try to see things through another's eyes. We can share and be generous and show gratitude and appreciation for each other. We can live within our means, and we can look out for each other. We can meditate and reinforce our connection with the Divine, with Ma'at. Maybe hugging a tree or attending a spiritual service helps us feel harmony. We can also establish our own traditions and values rather than adopt those values that the religion of our birth or our patriarchal consumer society tries to force on us.

We don't have to be cogs in their wheel or hamsters on a treadmill of excess, consumerism, and chaos. We can empower ourselves with awareness and knowledge, with the values of the Divine Mother, rather than the patriarchy, and teach that to our children. We can walk that talk and perpetuate it in our communities. We can demand it in our leaders. We can live by the laws of Mother Nature. She shows us that what we tend to and nurture survives and thrives, that things grow from the ground up. Growth does not trickle down. We can live in balance and harmony by the Mother's rules of interconnectedness and relatedness rather than the rules of rugged individualism and survival-of-the-fittest mentalities. We can realize we have finite resources and continual growth cannot be sustained and opt for the development of ourselves. We can re-adopt the ideal of the Jesus, aka the Sacred Masculine, who said, *"I tell you the truth, whatever you did not do for one of the least among you, you did not do for me."*

So, there is actually a lot we can do to bring more harmony into our lives and perhaps remember that sometimes chaos is our friend. So let us set our own boundaries and benchmarks. We are not the sheeple type. Get creative and share ideas. Dream outside the box. Create your own reality. Do not give in to fear or let it suck you into disharmony. We have road maps. Look to the caring cultures and values of matriarchies and carry those new traditions forward. With pride and certainty, perpetuate the way of the Mother, where we serve the whole, not just ourselves, where we live in harmony, valuing sharing and caring. Carry these ideals out with certainty that sanity, balance and order can reign in our lives. Be tenacious about embracing harmony. Be like water wearing away rock. We can restore the equilibrium and stop the run-away train. We can change the rules. We can be the change. Just think outside the box and embody or invoke the Goddess Ma'at and follow the innate abilities we have within us as children of the Sacred Feminine. We are here carrying the torch to reestablish her rules, so let us all be her messenger, her sacred roar, and remember, everything old is new again!

Chapter 9

Knowledge and Learning – Path to Goddess Wisdom

If you've listened to my radio show, *Voices of the Sacred Feminine,* you might have been tuned in on a night when I talk about the mission statement and mottos of the show. It goes like this:

As many of your know, adversaries of the Sacred Feminine tried to sweep away awareness and knowledge of Her for all time. With that sweeping away, when the Great She was made to disappear, women and their power, their leadership, their spiritual authority, were thwarted, repressed, and became taboo, diminished and disrespected because of the religion of patri-archy, of intolerant, selfish and power-hungry men, disconnected from Mother Nature and devoted to their war gods,. That's why on the show I'm dedicated to recovering the Great She, whether she be deity, archetype or ideal. Yes, we intend to defy, to taste the forbidden fruit, to be powerful and uppity women, to throw off the shackles, look under every rock and behind every locked door, and peer into the abyss of the past so we know why things are the way they are. How have things come to be turned on their head and so unnatural? And we're going to go about setting things right. Why? Because if we want to save ourselves as a species, I think we have no other choice. If we want to restore balance, harmony, wholeness, and sanity, it is women, armed with ideas of the Sacred Feminine, who will set things back on course. How do we start? We must be armed with our intuition and knowledge of what came before and what might be again. Knowledge is power. Not power *over*, but power for oneself, so you might be the best you can be.

And what about that knowledge? If you've been around Goddess Spirituality and Feminist Theology, you know it was pretty incredible finding what had been swept under the rug. You might liken it to being a **Diana Jones**, seeking out what had been *made to disappear* or what had been hidden. Did you know there was a name for who you are? You are the cognitive minority.

*"The cognitive minority is a group of people whose view of the world differs significantly from the one generally taken for granted in its society. It is the minority, considered offbeat by its contemporaries, that nearly always foresees the **true knowledge** of the future. And true knowledge is derived from a body of facts that will not go away, no matter how these facts may be interpreted or misinterpreted by the establishment. True knowledge is always a generation or two ahead of the disseminators of what is known as knowledge, that is, socially accepted knowledge."*

That comes from Elizabeth Gould Davis in her book, *The First Sex,* citing Peter L. Berger, author of *A Rumor of Angels.*

Remember when the Pagan scientists were trying to tell the Catholic Church the planets revolved around the sun and the Earth wasn't flat? They were the cognitive minority. Today, a contemporary example is the idea of Global Warming, separating those in the cognitive minority from the sheeple unable to accept true knowledge.

Maybe you've known about some other visionaries in the cognitive minority. I mention two of those devoted to true knowledge on my show as I use their quotes as the mottos of *Voices of the Sacred Feminine Radio.* The first is 19th century German Philosopher, Arthur Schopenhauer who says:

All truth passes through 3 stages. First, it is ridiculed. Second, it is violently opposed and third, it is accepted for being self-evident.

And the second is attributed to Gandhi:

First they ignore you. Then they laugh at you. Then they fight you. Then you win.

Let that soak in a minute. The next time you're apprehensive to speak out about the true knowledge of herstory, afraid of ridicule from the nonbelievers, remember you're in a select club. You're not one of the sheeple going along out of fear. You have the wisdom to be in the cognitive minority. You hold the true knowledge, and that makes you an important foremother or wayshower.

That said, let's think about where this knowledge resides, yesterday and today, namely in museums and libraries, the repositories of sacred knowledge.

When I was writing my first book, *Sacred Places of Goddess:108 Destinations*, I was very adamant that museums be considered sacred places. They are repositories of sacred knowledge. You could go into a museum, and no one could deny the existence and importance of Goddess and her spirituality. Like the Greeks, I too felt a place that was devoted to *learning and the arts* was a sacred place, a place where the Muses reside, otherwise known as a museum. And for a quick look at the 9 Muses, daughters of Mnemosyne and Zeus, and therefore Goddesses themselves, let us remember:

Calliope, She of the Beautiful Voice	– Muse of epic or heroic poetry
Sacred symbol	– writing tablet
Clio, The Proclaimer	– Muse of history
Sacred symbols	– laurel wreath and scroll
Erato, The Lovely	– Muse of love poetry and marriage songs, including the erotic
Sacred symbol	– lyre

Euterpe, The Well Pleasing	– Muse of music and lyric poetry
Sacred symbol	– flute
Melpomene, The Songstress	– Muse of tragedy
Sacred symbol	– tragic mask
Terpsichore, Whirler of the Dance	– Muse of dancing
Sacred symbol	– cymbal
Thalia, The Luxuriant	– Muse of comedy and idyllic poetry
Sacred symbol	– comic mask
Urania, The Heavenly	– Muse of astronomy
Sacred symbol	– globe and compasses
Polyhymnia, She of Many Hymns	– Muse of sacred song, dance, poetry, oratory, singing, and rhetoric
Sacred symbol	– veil

Speaking of the veil, there is an interesting inscription on the walls at the Temple of Sais, a medical school not far from Alexandria in ancient Egypt proclaimed by Plutarch to be a shrine of Athena, whom he identified with Isis. In this school of higher learning, attended by many female students and women faculty being taught gynecology and obstetrics, the aforementioned inscription on the wall reads:

"I am all that hath been, and is, and shall be: and my veil no mortal has hitherto raised."

Was Athena/Isis referring not to the exoteric teachings such as gynecology and obstetrics, but perhaps the esoteric, Divine

Mysteries, the knowledge of Her that lay behind the veil?

Another inscription that survives at this academy in Sais says:

"I have come from the school of medicine at Heliopolis and have studied at the women's school at Sais, where the divine mothers have taught me how to cure diseases."

Hmmmmm? Divine Mothers.

Before we leave these halls of knowledge of antiquity, it's fitting we not forget one of the most famous sacred shrines in all of the ancient world, the Library of Alexandria. I can tell you on good authority, much of the ancient knowledge we thought once lost in these libraries, we know has been saved and resides today, hidden in Christian monasteries throughout the Mediterranean region under the control of patriarchal religion, not unlike at the Vatican.

Speaking of the Library of Alexandria, it is being built anew today. Though the acquisitions are far from complete, the Bibliotheca Alexandrina is a major library and cultural center located once again on the shore of the Mediterranean Sea in the Egyptian city of Alexandria. It is both a commemoration of the Library of Alexandria that was lost in antiquity and an attempt to rekindle something of the brilliance that this earlier center of study and erudition represented. Interestingly, the International School of Information Science (ISIS) is a research institute affiliated to the new Bibliotheca Alexandrina. It acts as an incubator for digital and technological projects that nurture innovations in the spirit of the museum.

Indulge me one more minute on the subject of the Library of Alexandria. I strongly recommend viewing the 2009 Spanish film in English, *Agora,* about the life of the famous female and Pagan philosopher and mathematics professor, Hypatia. Watch how the cinematographer depicts the Christians storming the library, burning all the sacred scrolls of knowledge of the ancient world.

He literally turns the camera 360 degrees so you get a tangible sense of the world being turned on its head. The picture is worth not a thousand, but a million words!

Speaking of libraries or museums associated with or dedicated to the Sacred Feminine, we must pay tribute to Nashville's Parthenon which stands proudly as the centerpiece of Centennial Park, Nashville's premier urban park, with its recreation of the 42-foot statue of Athena as the focus of the Parthenon just as it was in ancient Greece. The building and the Athena statue are both full-scale replicas of the Athenian originals.

Of note is the wing of the Rosicrucian Museum in San Jose, CA, dedicated to the Egyptian Goddess, Sekhmet. In the Natural History Museum of Vienna, Austria, the Venus of Willendorf, has a very expensive wing dedicated to her, and she is one of their most prized, signature pieces that makes the museum famous. Of course the Met in NY, the Louvre in Paris, the British Museum in London and the Anatolian Museum in Ankara, Turkey are all wonderful sacred shrines of Goddess, but probably what surprised me the most were the many Goddess connections in Washington, DC, particularly, what I've come to call a temple of the Sacred Feminine, dedicated to knowledge, namely, the **Library of Congress**.

In the Grand Balcony, one can find Minerva, Nike and the Medusa, and throughout, female figures represent the sciences of botany, astronomy, chemistry, geology, mathematics, physics, zoology, and archaeology.

Attributes of courage, industry, temperance, fortitude, patriotism, prudence, and justice are embodied in feminine faces. Ideas of romance, history, tradition, erotica, lyrica, comedy, the five senses, the three graces, and the seasons are all represented in the Female form.

In the Southwest Pavilion, in the domed ceiling, the artist has depicted the four stages in the development of a nation: courage, valor, fortitude, and achievement. Each relates to a corresponding wall mural representing the historical sequence: adventure, discovery, conquest, and civilization. In this sequence, adventure leads to discovery, which in turn results in conquest, and finally civilization. All are embodied in the Female.

In the Reading Room, the Feminine represents philosophy, poetry, history, religion, art, science, commerce and law, and in the Reading Room's Great Dome, you look up and see a painting of a beautiful female figure, representing human understanding, in the act of lifting the veil of ignorance and looking forward to intellectual progress. She is attended by two cherubs: one is holding the book of wisdom and knowledge, and the other seems, by gesture, to be encouraging viewers beneath to persist in their struggle toward perfection.

And finally, in the Northwest Gallery, peace is represented in a religious procession. The inhabitants of a village have come to the border of a grove bearing on a platform the image of their guardian Goddess. The villagers carry various objects and lead a sacrificial bull to be offered as memorials to the Goddess in thanks for peace

Coming back full circle to where we began with the Muses, the Goddesses of the arts, learning and sacred knowledge, let us look at the Greek Goddess, Metis, who has had an asteroid and moon named after her in contemporary time.

According to Elizabeth Gould Davis in *The First Sex*, Metis is in earliest Greek mythology, the creative principle or female intelligence. Like Gaia, Anat, and Tiamat, she is the creator of all; at first all-female, then she becomes bisexual, a hermaphrodite, as in her title Metis-Phanes, creator and begetter in one body. Then in her final transformation by Classical Greek time, she becomes all male, Phanes, which scholars will say illustrates the ancient concept of the evolution of the human race. Elizabeth Gould Davis goes on to say:

"...for the original femaleness of all human beings is reflected in the

belief among the ancients, and voiced by Plato in the Symposium, that the human race was once unisexed, male and female combined in one self-perpetuating female body."

Interestingly, in the mythology of Zeus and Metis, Zeus feels the need to swallow Metis, his first wife, because he doesn't want her to birth a son that will come to defeat him. Now Metis is thought to be magical cunning, wisdom, wise counsel and knowledge. And this "swallowing" can be looked upon in many ways. Was there more to this swallowing than to prevent her from birthing a powerful son? Did he swallow her to co-opt her power as female, including her life-giving abilities, because remember, soon after he tricked Metis into becoming a fly and swallowed her, Zeus takes on the role of the female and births the patriarchal version of Athena from his head. This patriarchal version of Athena then gives all credit for her birth to Zeus. Metis remains within Zeus to continue to give him advice or wise counsel.

We know there was a time when women's roles in repro-duction were denied or questioned, and women's wombs became little more than an incubator for the male seed. So we have another story where we see it is so important to contemplate understanding, knowledge and truth. What were the Greeks trying to tell us – or what were they trying to obfuscate?

As we examine the many faces of Goddesses who represent learning and knowledge, let us also look at the archetype Metis once again through the eyes of Dr. Jean Shinoda Bolen. She believes Metis is the story of many of the first wives of successful men. The wife provides the ways or means so a man can get ahead, only to be cast aside later, receiving no credit for her efforts, or being "swallowed." Dr. Bolen says this also occurs in the work world when a "Zeus" takes credit for one's work or accomplishments.

On the flip-side, Dr. Bolen says Metis is a wise counselor, who uses time, energy, talents and resources in a judicious manner, so the wife will rebound. She believes Metis comes into your life when you are feeling powerful and don't have to dedicate all your energy to taking care of a husband, kids or family members. Metis can guide women through illness or loss and betrayal. She urges the use of introspection, solitude, meditation and therapy. She represents the gathering up of all your knowledge, wisdom, cunning, and skills. Metis would have you use your wise counsel for yourself. Reflect on your life and find who you are in midlife so you can yet still blossom and reinvent yourself. Doesn't this make you think about the multi-talented Super Mom who has employed so many skills during her lifetime as wife, mother and homemaker that she has all the talents necessary to be a CEO?

Goddess mythology has much to teach us, and the story of Metis teaches us not to hide our light under a bushe l– to not let ourselves be swallowed up or let another take credit for our gifts. To recognize all our abilities and put them to use for ourselves. Metis teaches us not to be afraid to let our own talents shine and receive accolades. As Elizabeth Gould Davis says, "The time has come to put woman back into the history books, to readmit her to the human race. Her contributions to civilization have been greater than man's, and man has overlooked her long enough."

Chapter 10

Crossroads and Pathways

When we think of the crossroads, we might think of that inter-section between life and death, where the veil between the worlds is thinnest. Hecate is standing there with her lantern, helping us see or feel that connection with our departed loved one on the other side. Yet there are many kinds of crossroads where Hecate is standing lighting the ways forward so we make progress, evolve and grow. To do that, we must take stock of where we are and where we're going because our lives are not meant to stagnate. It was Herodotus that said the sistrum, sacred instrument of Isis, Bast and Hathor, was shaken to keep the energies of the universe flowing. Yes, we also want the energies in our lives to move and dance, so they do not become mired down, immovable, stuck or dead. Water teaches us a similar lesson. Water not constantly moving becomes stagnant and unhealthy, where no life thrives.

However, that said, let us not dismiss the idea of marinating a bit at the crossroads, taking a deep breath before we step forward this way or that and grounding ourselves, getting our bearings, carefully considering before we begin to move ourselves, our life and our family and commit to a specific direction or goal. You certainly do not want to leap out of the frying pan and into the fire as my Mom used to say. You do not want to be impulsive or move for the sake of moving. Running willy-nilly, here and there without a plan or focus just for the sake of doing something, is not the best plan either.

Only you can check in with yourself and decide if you are stuck though, if you are being too complacent, if you are toler-ating a situation that is not working, or if you are perhaps in denial about the circumstances or not paying attention.

This means bad habits too. Are we stuck in the habit of not exercising? Eating too much sugar? Not eating our broccoli? Hanging around with toxic people who don't support and nurture us? Are we letting people fill our heads with donkey dung?

Are we stuck in a rut when it comes to our thinking and never evolving when new information comes our way to help us change? Liberals are fond of joking about the Right Wing bubble that facts don't penetrate, leaving those inside living in their own reality. The Broadway play, *The Book of Mormon,* highlighted this disconnect from reality when mentioning some of their irrational or nonsensical beliefs, but proudly, the singers explained, "Mormons just believe anyway."

Dare I say we have to be careful of the same thing? Yes, we are the cognitive minority, the ones blazing the trail of new thought (or old thought that's resurfaced and is new again) with our pink-handled machetes, but sometimes we might get stuck in patterns of thinking too.

Maybe it's about how our body looks. How do we see ourselves in the world? Do we have healthy self-esteem? How do we react to life's challenges? How do we habitually deal with our parents or siblings? How do we respond when we're questioned or judged? Are we separating the truth from the myths?

What we resist persists. When I heard that, I could immediately relate. It seems the Universe keeps sending similar challenges until you see what needs correcting and correct it. I'm no longer ashamed to say, about 20 years ago, I had self-esteem issues. I was told by a group of women that I was not their peer, their equal. I didn't stack up to them. For a time I let them define me. They beat me down so badly I was afraid of my own voice. Literally.

For quite some time during and after this, it seemed like everything, tarot readings, affirmation cards, situations with people, kept relating to issues of self-esteem. It caused me to dig out that metaphoric mirror and do some reflecting. At first it was, "Why does this keep happening to me?" In time I realized these challenges were defining me. The challenges literally caused me to ask myself if I knew who I was and wanted to be. Did I have something to say, and would I stand up and say it or become a hairball in the corner? In time I did find my path, my backbone, and realized those women were wrong. I had something to say and lots to offer. I wanted to be Her Sacred Roar. I was not going to be a sheeple, sitting at the feet of my oppressors. I was not going to conform to who they wanted me to be. I was going to find out who I was and how I might serve on my own terms. In that process I not only discovered myself, but I found out what I wanted in friends and community, too.

It was not easy. It didn't happen all at once. It was a process of pathways and holding patterns. Of course, there was the fear and pain of uncertainty at times. These women were my best teachers, and I believe I see Goddess' hand in those women's cruelty. They forced me to find myself. What did not kill me did make me stronger. I managed not to stay stuck, wasting myself and my potential. Sometimes we have to take a risk even if it's uncomfortable, because the devil we know is not always better than the devil we don't. I can relate to all these old clichés now.

Risk and choices. Those are always at the crossroads and pathways. My husband and I took a risk moving from New Orleans, leaving everything we knew. We left our friends, our jobs, and the neighborhoods we knew and grew up in, for the hope of something better. You have to calculate your risks. Obviously your choices have consequences, no matter what we're talking about: partners, spirituality, vacation destinations, your diet, career, friends. Maybe you know someone full of fear and disappointed because she never challenges herself. Most of the people I grew up with are like that. They live and die rarely traveling 50 miles beyond where they live. They exhibit no intellectual curiosity, no desire to live outside their box. My dear mother was a conundrum. She taught me to go out and get what I wanted, but she was very afraid when I left New Orleans. If it were up to her, I would never have stepped foot outside the United States. For some that might be living. For me, that would be a sure death by stagnation.

You really stand at a crossroads of sorts everyday whether you are conscious of it or not. In some aspect of your life, you will sit and marinate because it works perfectly for you. That might represent itself in a long-term marriage or partnership or city where you choose to live. It might represent a commitment to being in school and studying for a while to change careers. That's okay if this holding pattern is serving or nourishing you. I've had the same job for over 20 years, but it suits my purposes. I could make more money, have more status doing something else, but I choose to do what I do so I can feed my passions outside work. I see this as choosing a path that offers a certain quality of life over a path that might have provided more financial reward. We make these kinds of choices throughout our lives.

Just be sure to take stock periodically. Do uncomfortable patterns keep repeating themselves, calling for you to look at them and do something different? There's wisdom in that other cliché – the one about doing the same thing over and over and expecting a different outcome which is insanity. Check in. Do not get stuck in denial. Pay attention, and be self-aware. See if you have become mired down in something that is not good for you. You might realize it is time to take a leap of faith.

You have probably figured out I'm a movie buff and find some life lessons in films. Here's another one. Remember the Indiana Jones movie when he's standing before the chasm within that temple in Petra? He is, of course, terrified because he is being called to step where there is no visible path. Ever feel like that? Well, Indiana steps forward because he knows there is no going back, and suddenly a path presents itself. Life's crossroads and pathways might feel like that sometimes. New things always do.

So when you feel stuck, when you feel shoved, when you know something is not working, look for that beam of light Hecate is shining before you. You will find your way.

Chapter 11

Gratitude and Appreciation – Tending Your Garden

Gratitude and appreciation. In the times we are living in today, it might seem very hard to conjure up those feelings. Maybe we are full of fear, anger, jealousy, and disappointment. Well, we cannot let those feelings get the upper hand, especially because showing gratitude and appreciation is such a powerful magical tool of the cosmos. It is part of the equation of how the law of attraction works. What we focus on comes back to us because our thoughts are powerful tools of manifestation. So if we focus on lack of money or unpaid bills, guess what we manifest? If we focus on how miserable we feel, we'll continue to be down in the dumps and be in a bad mood. Gratitude, on the other hand, actually makes us feel wealthy!

So, be appreciative even if you feel there might be days when the only thing you have to be grateful for is your beautiful cat purring on your lap. There is nothing wrong with the love and serenity that will bring you. Really think about everything you do have to be grateful for and immerse yourself in the positive, gold, glowing feeling of gratitude and appreciation. You will attract to yourself more things to be grateful for, more feelings of true wealth. Be appreciative of the money you have, and more will come to you. Be appreciative of the love and good friends in your life, and more will come to you. And remember, the more you feel you have, the more you actually manifest; then you will have more to share with others, and the circle turns, because that is part of the power of the attraction equation. The circle of reciprocity turns as long as you feed it.

Be someone who defines themselves by their gratitude and their sharing. Be concerned for another and others will be concerned for you. We are not islands. We are all interconnected and depend on each other. Goddess teaches us our relatedness, not "survival of the fittest" individualism. Now this doesn't mean you have to be satisfied with what you have and can't want more than you might have already, but focus on gratitude for what you do have, not scarcity, and you will get back what you give.

So, you still feel as if your gratitude tank is low? Not feeling like life has smiled upon you? Well, let's take a look at what you might be seeking out and achieving. Is what you've been busy acquiring fulfilling you or leaving you feeling empty? After all, it *is* a challenge in this consumer-oriented world to strike a balance and not get caught up in society's measure of wealth. Be honest. Are you susceptible to the advertising? Must you have the latest electronic gadget? Does your phone plan include the secrets of the universe? Your co-worker's might! What about fashion? Are you wearing this year's hottest designs? How many pairs of shoes are in your closet? Do you trade in your car every year so it's always shiny and new but never paid for? Is your zip code famous? Do you own a house? Do you vacation on the Aegean or cruise along the Nile? Do you have a diploma from an Ivy League school? Do you have your stock broker's number on speed dial?

No doubt some of the above status symbols might open some doors or might offer some sense of pleasure or security, even a temporary measure of self-worth in our consumer-driven, materialistic culture, but as long as we're being honest, does it really bring you joy? When you lay in bed at night, do you have serenity and contentment? Do you feel fulfilled, or do you feel like a hamster on a wheel trying to keep up? Perhaps that is blocking your gratitude.

Let's take a look and see if you've been tending your personal garden or if it's in need of a big dose of Miracle Grow. It might be time for a reality check of your true wealth, and I don't mean the balance in your checkbook! Have you been so busy growing assets and nurturing your portfolio you've forgotten to water the garden that flowers true wealth? If so, maybe that's why you're not feeling filled with gratitude and appreciation.

Take stock right now. Don't wait, and don't allow yourself to slip into denial. Ask yourself these questions:

Do you know your neighbors? Could you call on them if you needed a ride to work or got sick? Research has been done showing how richer people have poorer social skills because they just hire people to do what they need.

How's your love life? Do you have a partner who truly loves you? When was your last date night? Do you express your love every day? Do you make a point not to go to bed angry?

What about your friends? Are they loyal, honest, reliable, trustworthy? Can they be counted on in a pinch? Are you there for them in equal measure? When was the last time you picked up the phone to see how they were doing and if they needed any help?

And the kids? When was the last time you got creative to deepen the bonds with your children? I know you're slammed, but when have you last shared together what's happening in your day?

How about your community? Do you have one? Does it feed you? Is there reciprocity? Are you there for others in need in your community? Do you expect them to be there for you?

Does your job fulfill you? How's your relationship with your co-workers? Do you communicate well with your boss? Have you baked a cake and brought it in for the people in your work life lately? Maybe your boss needs a nudge to take everyone out for a day of appreciation.

Have you thought about your relationship with God/dess lately? Had any meaningful connections? When was the last time you hugged a tree or stayed at the beach listening to the ebb and flow of her breath in the tides? Do you feel like the magic is missing in your life?

Are you feeding your passion? Are you nurturing yourself? Don't say you don't have time! If you don't nourish your passion, you will continue to feel like your gratitude tank is on empty.

Family can be complicated, but are you trying to be proactive when dealing with parents and siblings rather than reactive and playing out family dramas? Have you picked up the phone and called Mom and been patient with the woman on the phone who brought you into the world?

Worst-case scenario: If everything collapsed around you, do you have someone truly remarkable to call like a mentor, someone who can pull you up from the depths of despair. Are you there for them should the shoe be on the other foot?

Depending on how you answered these questions, you are probably realizing whether or not you have been tending to your real riches and why you do or don't feel filled with gratitude and appreciation.

Don't underestimate the small things that bring so much beauty and potency to our garden of riches. Are you taking for granted those jousting blue jays outside your window that entertain you or the hummingbirds that suckle on the beautiful flowers during your morning walk? What about delicious food or a fine museum in your city? Have you stopped to think about how grateful you are for those substantive conversations you have with friends that spark your creativity? What about the music on the radio? It's not just background noise. It can be a doorway to wonderful memories and feelings of intense inspiration, gratitude and appreciation. Are you grateful for your clients? Do you appreciate your freedom of speech and your ability to practice your own religion freely? Do you give thanks for your prosperity, opportunities or talents you possess?

Then there is health. If you are fortunate enough to have good health, do you appreciate it? Do you nurture it and feel gratitude for being able to climb that mountain path or for being able to dance to your favorite music? Do you fully enjoy the scent of your favorite perfume? The breathe itself is a gift that insures we are alive, and tomorrow brings the potential to start anew.

When you look into the night sky and see the face of Luna, are you happy for the feeling of wonder and mystery she might conjure or for the feeling of connection that might induce? Are you seeking out and soaking in the wealth Goddess gives us so freely and in abundance? If your answer is yes, then you are probably moving the needle to the full mark on your gratitude tank.

Now, while I still have your attention and this is fresh in your mind, I want you to make a commitment to do several things:

Jot down a list of ten things you are grateful for. I want you to fold it up and put it somewhere where you can reach it easily and often, and I want you to memorize it.

Next I want you to take a favorite piece of jewelry, maybe a bracelet or watch, that you can see throughout the day. Let this be your gratitude trigger. At least once a day, when you see your gratitude trigger, take a brief moment to remember something from your list you are grateful for. This is particularly important when times are tough and you're busiest. This way your attention and awareness will grow your riches and gratitude.

Take out your calendar and make a play date with the kids, a date night with your loved ones and a day just for yourself. Maybe read that book you have been thinking about reading in a bubble bath with scented candles.

Reach out to your friends and family. Send a notecard to those who have been there for you, even if it was months or years ago. Call a sibling, friend or co-worker and tell them about the lovely thing you remember they did for you. Show your appreciation.

Don't just let the gratitude be in your heart and mind; pay it forward. Put that positive intention out in the world, and watch it come back to you in how your cope and manifest. Make another's day by showing gratitude, and see if someone doesn't do the same for you.

Finally, let me make you a promise. There is a certainty that comes along as a side benefit of gratitude. Some might call it faith. Call it faith or certainty, you will have a life filled with joy, abundance and success. This certainty helps our emotional state when things seem insurmountable. It helps us stave off fear and other negative emotions. In the absence of gratitude and certainty, our pain might feel permanent causing us to focus on our physical lack or lack of confidence that we can resolve our problems. So be grateful. You want that certainty as your ally or antidote. Watch how it will bring you happiness, serenity, good health and abundance. Remember, don't waste energy on what you don't have. Focus your gratitude and appreciation on what you do have, and be certain it will grow exponentially in your life.

Chapter 12

Quest for Love and Wholeness

Many often consider the question, is the Divine male or female or both? Or is deity beyond gender altogether? The many answers to these questions have been cause for much argument, conversation, friction and oppression across the globe as women, transgenders and gays are diminished within patriarchal Abrahamic religions.

Looking back into the past of many cultures, we see the Divine Source embodied both the Masculine and Feminine. Ometeotl, an androgynous Aztec creator-deity, embodied the principles of the Divine Masculine, called Ometecuhtli, alongside the Sacred Feminine, or Omecihuatl. We often see images of the Hindu Goddess Parvati and the God Shiva embodied within one statue, with Shiva himself often depicted having very androgynous features. We have discovered statues of Aphrodite and Ishtar with male genitalia. The Greek Goddess, Metis started out as a female, then becomes bi-sexual – a hermaphrodite – as in her aspect as Metis-Phanes, a creator and begetter all in one body. If these deities are any example, it is clear gender exists in many forms, as do human beings.

Examining deities perhaps a bit more familiar to us in the West, we take a closer look at Aphrodite and Eros/ Cupid. Eros is sometimes thought of as the son of Aphrodite, but he is really an enigma. He is first mentioned as an early creation-god appearing alongside Gaia and Chaos. He is said to be hatched from the Egg of Night, the force that separated the two halves of the Cosmic Egg, or Heaven and Earth. Similar to Aphrodite's appearance at the birth of creation, *she and Eros are placed at the moment of disunion* of the cosmos. They are depicted as hermaphrodite beings, descended from the moon, sliced in half by Zeus, after which each half yearns and searches for the "other half" to be complete, their wholeness denied.

I was reminded of the dichotomy of love and disunion again as I walked through the Louvre Museum in Paris and gazed upon the famous statue of Hermaphroditus. Imagine for a moment you're in the City of Lights, certainly imbued with the essence of the Feminine. You're standing in the vast courtyard of the Louvre, about to descend beneath the glass pyramid that marks the entrance to this world renowned museum some would call a sacred site. As you walk through the galleries of statues, one in particular catches your eye. At first glance, one might easily miss the full potency of what the statue represents and the deeper meaning it might tend to convey. When you approach Hermaphroditus from her backside, she appears to be a beautiful woman lounging naked on a divan. Walking around the piece, looking from the front view, you see the woman also has male genitalia. Hermaphroditus never fails to elicit staring and whispers from museum-goers, with most never really learning the story behind this work of art or thinking beyond their immediate titillation.

Hermaphroditus was the son of Mercury and Venus. When the boy was 15, he and the nymph Salmacis were so in love with one another that they prayed they would never part. Hearing their plea, the gods took action, and when the pair embraced, the two became fused as one, with a body both male and female.

While some just see this as a simple story of two young lovers, there are varying ways to look upon this and the aforementioned myths if we want to mine the depths of the symbols and meaning within these ancient love stories. Of course some may think this was punishment for their lust and desire. Some see this joining of Hermaphroditus and Salmacis as simply a reflection of "every man and woman". Or they might imbue their joining with deeper meaning and see them as embodying Divine Order and Balance. Still they might represent the ultimate symbol of the hieros gamos or Sacred Marriage, the divine mystery of procreation, our life force, later deemed corrupting taboo or as sin in the Bible.

The joining of Salmacis and Hermaphroditus, like Parvati and Shiva, Aphrodite and Eros or Ometecuhtli and Omecihuatl, could be looked upon as representative of the true and natural essence of the Divine Source, which embodies both the Divine Masculine and Feminine, together as THE ONE.

Taking that a step farther, both woman and man, whether joined together or in their divine separateness, were both equally created in the image of the Supreme Being. Only the Judeo-Christian patriarchs conveniently omitted half of the spiritual equation from their creation myths as they sought to elevate man above woman and unbalance the natural order within creation. Patriarchy's choice of disunion and disharmony is seen by many as the catalyst creating the chaos and negative reverberations heaped upon us today for having swept the Sacred Feminine from the world stage and from so many human psyches.

On a personal level, the stories of Aphrodite and Eros and Salmacis and Hermaphroditus certainly reminded me a great deal of each person's continual yearning for love and their burning desire to be enveloped within love's womb of warmth. This seeking might be referred to as unrequited love or the search for our soul mate or other half.

These bi-sexual and hermaphrodite deities certainly give us much food for thought as they reflect many ideas and challenge the dogma of society and religious institutions. They speak to the necessity for each of us to not just find love or completion from another, or outside ourselves, but that all important source of self-love, where it lives within, even if it might be buried deep. It reflects the importance of embracing wholeness, sometimes referred to as the balance of masculine and feminine within ourselves, and in doing so, means giving ourselves permission to be fluid in our masculinity and femininity. That realization would allow humankind to follow their heart and embrace their most authentic self without society seeing a masculine woman or a feminine boy as worthy of ridicule. It might mean looking upon persons born a hermaphrodite or transgendered as just another divine ingredient in our sacred human stew, rather than an abnormality. After all, some cultures see transgendered persons and their unique and close association with both sexes as closer to the Divine Source.

These deities embodying both genders in partnership within themselves challenge the religious dogma of sexism, homophobia and discrimination. Recognizing these deities as role models or archetypes, no longer would attributes of the Feminine be considered less than, weak or devalued, and by association, neither would women or effeminate men. Just one consequence might lead to women never again being denied their calling to spiritual authority because of their genitals.

Quite simply, if one can see virtues of equality, partnership, inclusiveness, wholeness, acceptance, tolerance and love embodied in these deities who are both masculine and feminine, with all the attributes associated with each gender, is it not the challenge of humanity to find these qualities within ourselves? Then, after embodying these values in ourselves, being truly comfortable in our own skin, is it not our human responsibility to look outside ourselves and strive to have empathy and love for another?

Chapter 13

Separating Truth from Myth

Once you realize how the feminine face of god was swept beneath the sands of time, you begin to realize what passes for truth, history and myth is written by the conquerors or those in power, often for their own agenda. Many examples come to mind.

What we know about Cleopatra comes mostly from her enemies. Can we truly have an accurate picture of this powerful and resourceful woman? And what about all the women whose accomplishments never make the history books? We are constantly reminded of that when we see the dearth of women's history during Women's History Month. Goddess Advocates do not believe the myth of the Egyptian Goddess Sekhmet actually conveys her true essence and story. They theorize the myth of this Goddess being a mercenary for her father, the Sun God, Ra, is clouded in a patriarchal purpose, perhaps as a story to fear women or for women to fear their own power. Mary Magdalene was thought to be a prostitute for centuries, and that story was rather quietly corrected only a few decades ago. The Goddess Athena, in patriarchal times, is birthed not from her mother, Metis, but from the head of Zeus. We can see how even natural laws are turned on their head when those with the leisure, authority or power are writing the story. And these stories have important consequences in society.

Think about how the Church silenced science and jailed men who would tell us the Earth revolved around the Sun or how the new Christian beliefs taking hold in the world diminished women and led us into the Dark Ages. It wasn't only women who were victimized. What about the destruction of the cultures of the Hawaiians, Native Americans and Aztecs, to name a few closer to home on our continent.

In America we have our own versions of history. No doubt some Americans turn a blind eye to our county's influence abroad or see that influence one way, while the countries feeling the might of our heavy hand would tell a different story. In my short lifetime, many still question the truth behind the assassination of President John F. Kennedy, whether anyone in our government had advance knowledge of the bombing of Pearl Harbor or our government's collusion in the fall of the twin towers on September 11th.

When you realize how history can be fluid and truth slip between our fingers like drops of water, then we have an obligation to try to separate truth from myth. How many people still believe Saddam Hussein was responsible for 9-11? How many deny the science of global warming? What about those responsible for writing children's history books in Texas wanting to omit the writings of Thomas Jefferson and liberal or African American personages because Conservatives prefer to have these contributions and ideas hidden from developing minds? Likewise, the George W. Bush library in Texas is busy going about distorting the facts about the Iraq War. Will enough people remember the facts of the last decade, or will truth be lost over time?

What's missing from the history books? Truth and myth seem to always be in flux thanks to those with the time and money to rewrite history to their advantage, like those patriarchs who would give men the life-giving capabilities possessed only by women or Abrahamic religions that would do away with those heathens revering Goddess. Remember the destruction of the Library in Alexandria? So too did the real history of the indigenous people of America become romanticized and lost as Puritan imperialism set out to conquer the Indians and grab their land.

As we sit down each Thanksgiving to give thanks for our

bounty, it would probably be important to recognize that those sentiments of gratitude did not originate with the Pilgrims. Instead they had long been part of the paradigm of the indigenous people who relied so heavily on Mother Earth for their sustenance long before the Puritans arrived on the continent. In fact, it was the generosity, hospitality and gift-giving of the Indians that kept the Pilgrims alive when they arrived in America ill-equipped to sustain themselves.

So while Thanksgiving has become an important symbol of cooperation among people, Americans must face that that peace between the Pilgrims and Indians was short-lived. In fact, the purpose of the gathering on that first Thanksgiving was to negotiate a treaty that would secure the lands of the Plymouth Plantation for the Pilgrims, and possibly out of a sense of charity toward their hosts, it was the Indians who brought the majority of the food: five deer, wild turkeys, fish, beans, squash, corn soup, corn bread and berries. Indian women and men sat together to eat with the Pilgrim men, while Pilgrim women stood quietly behind the feasting table, awaiting their men to finish their meal before they might partake of the feast.

It might be stunning to realize who the Pilgrims actually were: political revolutionaries who intended to overthrow the government of England, who came to the new world to establish the Kingdom of God as foretold in the book of Revelation. When they realized they could not impose their "Rule of Saints" strict Puritan orthodoxy on the British people, they came to America over time in hundreds of ships with the intent to build their "Holy Kingdom." They saw themselves as the "chosen elect" and used any means, including deceptions, treachery, torture, slavery, war and genocide, to achieve their goals. These people were not the stuff of Hollywood's pilgrims or mythology's "Noble Civilization versus the Savages." They were rigid fundamentalists, and anyone who wasn't with them was against them.

Consider the Thanksgiving sermon delivered at Plymouth in

1623 by Mather the Elder who gave thanks for the smallpox plague which wiped out the majority of the Wampanoag Indians who had been their teachers and benefactors. Mather thanked God for destroying the children and young men which he considered the "seeds of increase, thus clearing the forests to make way for a better growth", i.e., the Pilgrims. The very people who had been their salvation, feeding them and teaching the Pilgrims the agricultural ways of the region so they might survive, were in actuality exploited and viewed as instruments of the Devil. In time the Pilgrims displayed the same intolerance toward the Indians and their religion that they displayed toward the less popular religions in Europe. Relationships deteriorated. Trust was lost. It was the beginning of the end for the generous indigenous people who welcomed the Pilgrims with opened arms. Within 50 years, the Wampanoag tribe so instrumental in helping the Pilgrims get a foot-hold was extinct.

It might be interesting to note that about 150 years later, Benjamin Franklin invited one of the indigenous tribes of the region, the Iroquois, to Albany, NY, to explain their democratic system of government to the country's forefathers. The forefathers were so impressed by what the Iroquois taught them, they developed the "Albany Plan of Union," a document which served as a model for the Articles of Confederation and Constitution of the United States. Notable too, among the Iroquois, women held the deciding vote in many important matters, and both genders enforced the laws of the village and helped solve problems. Yet, how many Americans know this version of history? Most of the Native Americans probably do. They know better than most non-Native Americans the history of the Trail of Tears and the devastation brought upon their culture by Christian-run Native American boarding schools.

So let us be very careful when we think we know our ancestors and our history or even what's happening in our present. Let us not be captivated by propaganda, romanticism or the movie-making of Hollywood, or particularly, the patriarchal conquerors who would rewrite history for the sake of their legacies as they whitewash their misdeeds, greed and exploitation. Let us forever be vigilant to seek out the untold story lest we celebrate falsehoods and sanitized versions of history across the globe.

Chapter 14

Compassion

Compassion is sometimes an elusive quality in today's capitalist and technological society. Too many adopt a "survival of the fittest" mentality, detaching from those around them, denying or ignoring we are all interconnected. Some never learn to have compassion for themselves much less another, rationalizing lack of empathy with ideas like "poverty is punishment" from their authoritarian God. Fortunately we have parables and mythology in place to help teach us, enlighten and uplift our spirits, and nourish our souls, and we have become familiar with these various deities, prophets, role models and avatars of compassion.

The Buddhist Goddess, Kwan Yin, quickly comes to mind with one of her famous pilgrimage sites of Pituoshan Island in the East China Sea. Reverence for Kwan Yin, Goddess of Mercy, crosses cultural and religious boundaries in both the East and West. As she pours forth from her vase the waters of compassion, she has comforted many and helped keep the essence of the Sacred Feminine alive for humankind.

Whether he was a genuine deity, messiah or prophet, thoughts may turn to Jesus. Certainly a rebel of his time, Jesus bucked convention as he mingled among those on the fringe of society. We all remember the angry confrontation in the Temple of the Money Changers as he rebuked the status quo, as he embraced the down-trodden, walked with and taught women, as he healed the sick and tried to teach love and compassion. Many can separate Jesus' teaching from the divisive dogma of religious institutions and try to emulate his words and deeds.

In the mortal realm, there is Florence Nightingale, a British woman of the Victorian era, who felt divinely called, resulting in her elevating nursing from the untrained ministrations of camp followers to the status of professional nursing we enjoy today. Florence, an English feminist who felt women of her time led wasted and lethargic existences, shattered societal mores becoming an inspiration for nurses coming after her, from the Civil War to the wars in which we are currently engaged. Perhaps best known for her soothing the suffering of soldiers, she had many achievements, including beginning the Women's Medical College in 1869.

More contemporary models of compassion are Mother Theresa and the Dalai Lama. Mother Theresa, known as the "Saint of the Gutters" held to her breast the indigent, the lepers, the forgotten and what some might call the scabs of society. Her selfless care of the sick and dying in India garnered attention worldwide. Though sometimes a controversial figure when it came to the sources of her donations and not upgrading her facilities to alleviate more suffering, the most powerful and influential would make time to speak with Mother Theresa and heed her requests. She was quoted as saying, "The poor do not want your bread, they want your love; the naked do not want your clothes, they want human dignity." Mother Theresa won countless awards, including the Nobel Peace Prize. By 1969 she was operating 517 missions, 755 homes and over 1350 clinics in more than 120 countries. Upon her death, the prime minister of France, Jacques Chirac sadly stated, "This evening, there is less love, less compassion, less light in this world."

Within Buddhism, an unenlightened life is suffering, thus a fundamental basis of this spirituality included understanding and developing the need for compassion for all things. The Dalai Lama, a Tibetan Buddhist monk, believed to be the contemporary living incarnation of the male aspect of the Bodhisattva Kwan Yin, has spoken much on the subjects of living a life dedicated to serving others, of being open-hearted and practicing compassion. He talks of transforming pride into humility and anger into love.

We might think of it as letting go of our "Us vs. Them" attitudes because we are all part of a whole. He believes women make better leaders because of their potential for compassion and has even stated publicly he believed it would be Western women who would save the world. He has made many profound statements on compassion which offer humanity guidance and wisdom, such as:

"Each of us in our own way can try to spread compassion into people's hearts. Western civilizations these days place great importance on filling the human brain with knowledge, but no one seems to care about filling the human heart with compassion. This is what the real role of religion is."

"Love and compassion are necessities, not luxuries. Without them humanity cannot survive."

"Our prime purpose in this life is to help others. And if you can't help them, at lease don't hurt them."

"I believe all suffering is caused by ignorance. People inflict pain on others in the selfish pursuit of their happiness or satisfaction. Yet true happiness comes from a sense of peace and contentment, which in turn must be achieved through the cultivation of altruism, of love and compassion, and elimination of ignorance, selfishness, and greed."

Within Kabbalah too, compassion, sharing, empathy, and the importance of having compassion are vital to living a good life and being a spiritual and successful person in the world.

We've seen human compassion in action as people mobilize and respond to disaster: Think about Hurricanes Katrina and Sandy, the Tsunami in Asia, 9-11, the nuclear disaster in Japan, tornadoes in Oklahoma and the Boston Marathon explosion. Can anyone forget the outpouring of compassion when Lady Diana passed over?

But what about applying compassion when it is really hard?

What about when doctors are indifferent to their patient's suffering? They say many doctors have to be taught compassion when they treat their patients without empathy.

Can you practice compassion when you're afraid of being scammed by people you suspect are pretending to be homeless or who may take your hard earned money to buy drugs or alcohol instead of food?

What about when you don't donate because you're worried the money is not going to those who are actually suffering but to pad the nest of the founders of the organization?

Can you have compassion for terrorists when you understand their only education might be religious indoctrination and hate theology?

What about when the fundamentalists attack Goddess and say non-Christians don't deserve to have the same religious freedoms or protections as Christians, or when they call the Queen of Heaven a demon? Can you get past their intolerance and ignorance with compassion?

Is it hard to muster compassion for people who push your buttons or make destructive choices? Who has not had to muster compassion sitting around the dinner table at Thanksgiving or when watching a family member in a destructive spiral? Yes, that's when you really get the credit, the Light, Her grace, when you practice compassion when it is not easy but because it is the right thing to do. Ultimately it's about putting out the right energy into the world. It sets a tone. Remember the Laws of Attraction. What you put out comes back to you, both good and bad, compassion, love, and tolerance or jealousy, indifference, and hate.

Remember our thoughts are things that can actually shape our reality and our lives. So it is very important to be aware of these concepts, universal, scientific, or spiritual. We literally shape our lives and our futures, so we must be aware and try our best, even with all of our mortal imperfections, as we to try to uplift ourselves and act with compassion and wisdom.

So to close, if you're in the mood for a field trip, how about experiencing the essence of the Goddess of Compassion and Mercy at your local Buddhist temple or Chinatown? But first, some temple etiquette:

When visiting many such temples, it is appropriate to bring an offering such as a fresh fruit or incense. Go before the statue; perhaps you can kneel before her altar and speak to her. She hears your anguish, your worries and your pain. She is also glad to hear your thanks and gratitude. She offers you comfort and serenity. This is the reciprocity of the Goddess.

Sometimes, visitors may avail themselves of a unique and powerful service provided by some temple clergy. You may ask the residing caretaker or minister to endow a devotional icon or statue with aspects of Goddess. This step should be taken only with the utmost consideration because it comes with great responsibility. Those devoted to Kwan Yin or her Taoist aspect, Tien Hau, believe once this act is performed, the Goddess resides within the statue and must be cared for and tended daily.

If after serious consideration you still wish to embark upon this commitment, bring your own deity statue and ask the priest or priestess to invite the spirit of Goddess to live within it. It will be necessary to leave the statue overnight when clergy will perform a ritual to accomplish this. Upon returning the next day to collect the statue or icon, the devotee may be instructed to place the image in a place of reverence and to attend to her daily by leaving fresh water or offerings such as a flower, incense or prayer. Even if you are not instructed to do so by the clergy, it is understood you are aware of this necessity. Of course a donation to the temple is customary for this service. This practice is common in the Hindu faith, and ancient Egyptians also believed deities resided in the statuary of home altars and temples alike.

Chapter 15

Hope and Fearlessness

Hope is one of those words that's a noun and a verb. It is both an action and a thing.

When hope is a noun, it can be the feeling that what is wanted can be had or that events will turn out for the best. Remember the feeling when you got that job? Hope can be a person or thing in which expectation is centered. We can probably all remember the slogan of the Obama campaign: Hope and Change.

When hope is a verb, it means to look forward to with desire and confidence, to believe, desire or trust, to feel that something desired may happen or to hope against hope.

Perhaps you may be aware that for years now, we have been living in a climate of fear which tends to thwart hope and instead brings about feelings of hopelessness and vulnerability. We hear about Global Warming, war, economic uncertainty, the housing bubble, corporate fascism, disaster and predatory capitalism, austerity, erosion of our civil liberties, the decline of the country and super viruses. It seems non-stop sometimes.

Dare I say, the powers that be often encourage that fear with talk of World War III or the End Times. We hear suggestions to get plastic and duct tape to keep us safe from terrorist attacks or are exposed to color coded terror alerts raising and lowering our awareness, keeping us off-balance and on an emotional roller-coaster. When we are constantly receiving these pictures and taking in these words and thoughts, our clarity becomes distorted, and we become more easily manipulated. We feel afraid. Then from a fearful place, we look for the white knight who can ride in and save us.

I'm going to suggest to each of you today you are your own white knight and must find your own sacred roar. You might do that by embodying the essence of one of our warrior Goddesses like Sekhmet, Kali, the Morrighan, or the Hindu God, Ganesh, known as the Remover of Obstacles.

Absent are public leaders and heroes who might instill hope within us, telling us or our children that we are powerful, we are capable, we have nothing to fear but fear itself, so we have to become our own hero or heroine and speak and practice empowerment ourselves. We have to value ourselves and step forward into fearlessness, removing the obstacles that prevent us from doing so. Perhaps that means creating a community of support. It might mean being a trailblazer yourself, even if you're afraid, because your action, your fearlessness, your trying, is contagious and gives another permission to try. Remember how the Occupy Movement and the Egyptian Spring encouraged others to mimic their actions?

But I'm not just talking about politics. I'm talking about stretching ourselves, challenging ourselves, trying to accomplish things we might feel are a bit beyond us. It is a journey of becoming and of growing we all must take, and we cannot be afraid of the journey. It's the journey that steels us. It is the trying, the praying, the stumbling and picking yourself back up, the seeking, the very *act of doing* that staves off fear and fills us with hope. The destination doesn't necessarily hold the reward. The reward comes from that which has been gleaned from the journey. The destination is just where you take a deep breath, reflect and relax **after** the journey has molded you. It's where we take a respite before beginning again to meet the next challenge or climb the next mountain.

Sometimes, as we get older, we naturally become more fearless. We've weathered a lot of storms, and we are not so easily daunted. We've had successes. We've learned we can survive defeat or disappointment. We might be more willing to try new things, to throw the spaghetti against the wall and see what might stick. And if we are fortunate enough to be in that place of empowerment, of feeling fearless, it might be a good thing to help those around us to believe in themselves, too. We might actively encourage and support one another, rather than compete or diminish one another.

Forget the empty platitudes and distractions. I will not recommend shopping to ward off bad things happening. I'm going to give you a few options that you can carry forward with you into your everyday life that might be useful tools or a springboard for your own ideas to keep yourself inspired and cultivating hope to keep fear and hopelessness at bay. And soon, if you take baby steps, it will become a part of your psyche and your new paradigm. You will find yourself rising to challenges more easily, meeting bigger and bigger challenges with less and less fear and trepidation, and you will not be so easily duped, confused or manipulated into hopelessness or apathy again.

First, let's understand the logic of these negative emotions and remember, we have to work against our brain's programming, and that's all it is. The fear impulse, that reaction, sometimes keeps us safe, but it often has nothing to do with logic.

According to Daniel Gilbert, Harvard University psychology researcher, "Negative emotions such as fear, hatred and disgust tend to provoke behavior more than positive emotions such as hope and happiness do." Guess that's why we hear about so many bullies rather than humanitarians.

Edmund Burke, 18th century political theorist observed, "No passion so effectually robs the mind of all its powers of acting and reasoning as fear." Does that explain why some of the powers that be might want to keep us on that rollercoaster of fear and perpetuate hatred of The Other – the brown or black skinned person, the Muslim, the gay man, the immigrant, the labor union, the French, the Welfare Queen, or science?

Then we must act to transcend the fear. There are many coping mechanisms you might put in your self-help tool kit:

- Contemplate Goddess or God, like Sekhmet and Ganesh, and amplify your connection to them.
- Use breathing techniques or physical activity to ward off anxiety and fear.
- Don't underestimate a good night's sleep. Everything looks better in the morning light.
- Learn to meditate. Walking meditations help relieve stress for me.
- Recall images, success or thoughts and memories that make you feel powerful and capable.
- Turn off the television, stop listening to the fear mongering and go outside!
- Arm yourself with knowledge so you can dispel fear and make the best possible decision or take the best possible action. Always look at the agenda of the fear-monger.
- Do not let fear of imperfection stop you from doing what you feel you are called to do!
- Write out your feelings in a journal, including the success of your coping mechanisms.
- Share your new found skills and knowledge with others to help empower them.

Visualizations are also great. There's a reason athletes are trained to see themselves achieving their goals. If you'd like to amplify your connection with empowerment deities, such as Sekhmet, begin to contemplate her. See yourself as her as your/her laser eyes dissolve obstacles to health, success or hope. See yourself atop the back of the elephant-god, Ganesh, as his powerful trunk is obliterating obstacles. Hold a smooth stone in your hand that has been weathered by water. Think of yourself as water wearing away rock, never giving up, but slowly achieving your goal.

Silly as it sounds, imagine yourself a super hero or heroine. Many of them have no super human powers beyond their cunning and will. A visual I like to recollect when I need a boost are two scenes from *The Lord of the Rings* movies. The first was when the Wizard stood alone on the edge of the precipice facing a huge and terrifying monster. I'm sure he was scared, but he mustered up all of his will and determination. He eye-balled the monster, stamped his staff upon the ground, and with certainty and confidence in his voice, he commanded that beast, "You shall not pass!" I don't know if that scene was powerful for you, but it still makes the hair stand up on the back of my neck.

The battle scene in the third *Lord of the Rings* movie inspired me where this soldier is battling a monster. The monster tries to psyche the soldier out and instill fear and hopelessness, saying *he cannot be killed by man.* The next scene was quite a surprise to everyone. Undaunted by the monster's threats of superiority, the soldier's helmet comes off, you see the soldier is a woman, and she tells him, *"I am not a man!"* Then she slays the monster dead.

Often it is our very demeanor that determines outcome. Do we move forward boldly, perhaps hiding our trepidation, or do we outwardly show our self-doubt in word and deed? Confidence or doubt is an energy we exude, and it can be perceived. How often do you hear heroines say, "Of course, I was afraid, but I did what I had to do anyway." Underdogs do win. Guerrilla fighters can defeat the Death Star. Adversaries can smell fear, so wear your best perfume when you must stand up and be fearless!

Of course I'm talking in metaphor, but these are symbolic of struggle and challenge where we must dig deep and find within us the means to hope and fearlessness. When we do, the Universe, She of Ten Thousand Names, often rewards us in ways we might not imagine. You might say, "Audentes Fortuna iuvat," or the Goddess Fortuna favors the bold! And finally, and maybe most important, when we no longer fear death or endings, when we accept both as part of an inevitable cycle, metaphorically or otherwise, then we are truly liberated!

Chapter 16

Trusting in the Journey

If I were to sit down and have a heart-to-heart with a young person or student, even one of my peers, I would tell them, above all, when planning your career or personal life, it is vital to *trust in the journey*. Far too often we obsess on the destination or the goal. Maybe you want to own our own business, get married or start a family. Perhaps you want to publish a book or see your play performed on Broadway. We all have goals for financial security. Maybe we just want to find our life's purpose.

I started to take this idea in when I started planning actual journeys or sacred pilgrimages. I realized the journey began long before our plane touched down in a foreign land. The journey began when we got the first inkling we might be interested in traveling or in visiting a sacred site of a particular Goddess. Time passed. We learned more and more. Desire, curiosity, our calling all developed. Perhaps we had to manage our budget and cut corners to afford the journey. We honed our skills at meditation, sensing energies, or noticing our dreams, so we might be better prepared for all the sacred site might impart. Perhaps we learned the language of the country we planned to visit or researched the political climate or social customs.

Then we arrive, despite all our preparation, we are thrown into a new place. The money is different. The people may dress different. The sounds, smells, and energy of the place are all foreign. We feel like a fish out of water, yet the journey continues to mold who we are, how we react, and what we learn. All this while we have been changing, we've been trusting in the journey.

We dream and vision, work and plan. Then life sometimes has a way of throwing us off course, and we take a detour. Sometimes it is a single detour; other times it may be multiple unexpected twists, turns or what might be perceived as setbacks. It might be one step forward and two steps back. It might seem as if our goal is ever more elusive, and we worry about achieving success. In our focus to grasp that brass ring, what we might be missing is who we are becoming and what we are learning on the journey. We might not be aware of the skills, insight and wisdom we are picking up along the way. What might look like a disappointment at first glance might soon reveal itself to be a blessing in disguise. These challenges were steps in the process to ready you for the next phase of the journey. Sometimes we realize our vision for a plan must adjust, and we must shift gears and see it manifest in another way.

When one trusts in the journey, rather than lamenting that partnership that does not work out, you may be opening the way for the right collaboration. The rejection letter from a publisher might cause you to hone your skills and write a better proposal. A marriage that fails may reset the circumstances for you to find your soul mate. The lover you left because he cheated on you was saving you from more grief. A business that might not be thriving may cause you to revision your business plan, even rethink your life goals. Maybe you wanted to open a flower shop or become an actor and not be an accountant anyway! That job you lost might set the stage for you to go back to school or follow your life's passion.

I have in hindsight seen what I call the hand of Goddess in the most difficult of life's challenges, even when in the thick of the adversity, I could not see it was Hecate's lantern showing the way.

What I first deemed the end of the world, a tragedy, was really a new beginning. These challenges have helped teach me tenacity and self-worth. I've learned not to cast my pearls before swine. Through trial and error, I recognize what I want in friends and community and what I most definitely reject. I have come to know who I am and what I believe in. I know I value loyalty, reciprocity, tolerance and supportive friends and strive to embody all those things. I reject discrimination and fight for equality because I have felt the stab of that injustice thrust upon me. I have discovered that I do not have to be perfect and have all the answers before starting something I feel called to do. Allies show up, and questions are answered. Never underestimate on-the-job-training! It is a lot like trying to manifest something. You do everything you can to make it happen. You recognize your connection to the beneficent universe, our great Mother Goddess of abundance and magic. You acknowledge you are worthy of good things coming your way. You take steps to help manifest it in the material world. Then you watch for the doors to open and the signposts to appear along the way. Just be careful what you wish for, as the saying goes, because you might just get it.

Of course that might sound like an over-simplification for how one should go through life, but is it? Once you've ridden life's rollercoaster a few times and have managed to take the ups and downs with a sense of adventure rather than in white-knuckled fear or wide-eyed bewilderment, you start to recognize how your certainty and trust in the process can have a remarkably positive influence on the outcome. You start to see the serendipity and magic. You look for the gifts in the challenges. You realize you are a beautiful thread in a magnificent tapestry, and you relax into not being privy to how this masterpiece will look upon its completion. You just have to surrender to the fact you are a work in progress, and so is your life, and the road traveled will be one of wonder even if your plans and final destination change course along the way.

Chapter 17

Resistance is Not Futile

Before Ayn Rand became a household name or Michael Douglas as Gordon Gekko in the movie, *Wall Street*, captivated the masses with his "greed is good" ideals, giving license to callously cheat and exploit, we believed in the progressive values of the movies and television series, *Star Trek*. Remember, in *Star Trek II: Wrath of Khan* (1982) when Mr. Spock's dying words to Captain Kirk were "the needs of the many outweigh the needs of the few." A few years later, in *Star Trek: First Contact* (1996), Captain Picard explains their world view in the future when he says, "The acquisition of wealth is no longer the driving force in our lives. We work to better ourselves and the rest of humanity." In fact, *Star Trek's* mission was one of exploration and humanitarianism rather than the Right Wing rejection of science and modernity or the Ayn Rand values to spurn collectivism and altruism.

That said, I wonder how many have considered how much more Trekkies and Goddess Advocates have in common? Let's see.

Let's start with how Goddess ideals are about the "We and the Us" rather than the "I and Me." Sounds synonymous with the aforementioned words of Spock, does it not? Goddess Advocates have talked about a gift economy rather than the predator capitalism of Gordon Gekko which causes vast income disparity and massive suffering of the 99%.

Women certainly were equal in the world of *Star Trek*, as they are in Goddess Spirituality. Sexism, vaginal probes or pay inequity would not be a reality in Earth's future á la Gene Roddenberry, creator of *Star Trek*. Number One, the early Science Officer before Mr. Spock, comes to mind, as does Janeway, Captain of the Enterprise. Women were allowed to break out of traditional roles, and never did I see an episode where the church or the state dictated women's rights.

Goddess, by her many names and faces across the globe is the poster girl for diversity and tolerance. Think back to Captain Kirk and Uhura's first interracial kiss and the multi-cultural *Star Trek* crews throughout the series. In fact, Earth was part of The Federation of Planets which existed under a central government based on principles of universal liberty, rights and equality. Planets shared their resources in cooperation as in how the assistance from the Vulcans enabled Earth to lift itself out of poverty and suffering after World War III. You did not see all this fear or devaluation of The Other.

With our finite resources, we can no longer continue to exploit Gaia. We must reject unfettered growth and opt for the development of our species. In Earth's future, *Star Trek* suggested humans were left to pursue their passions and become the best version of themselves they might become. Considering planets shared resources, I cannot imagine in *Star Trek* multinational corporations would be allowed to continue to exploit the masses. In fact, the resources of Gaia would probably become free. Imagine not paying for electricity or gas and multinational corporations prevented from poisoning or stealing water from indigenous people.

Remember the Prime Directive? The *Star Trek* crew was not to interfere with the development of cultures they discovered. There were no crusades, inquisitions, missionaries or religious institutions forcing their dogma on people or the State as the one true way, nor was there any legislating of a certain religious conformity. Captain Kirk did not beam off the ship and say, "We'll help you if you accept Jesus as your savior," or "We'll give aid if you teach sexual abstinence as the only form of birth control."

I'm sure this will get you thinking of the many episodes of morality within the long-running and beloved *Star Trek* series.

One that stands out for me was when Captain Kirk and his crew encountered two groups of peoples who were at war. The skin of one species was black on the right and white on the left and the other people had skin white on the right and black on the left. As they battled each other for supremacy, each devaluing the other, viewers were encouraged to see the folly of racism in our time and think about how society treated minorities.

There were many such episodes, and the social and cultural issues presented by Gene Roddenberry are still ones we wrestle with today, but somehow, the scripts taught us to challenge our thinking and appeal to the better angels of our natures, rather than discrimination, fear, exploitation, and greed. The world was not perfect, but there was a solidarity among peoples and a sense their priority was the common good.

What was your favorite episode? What values did *Star Trek* teach you or your kids? How did the series make you feel as you saw the bravery and selflessness of the crew, often risking themselves for others? Were they your heroes and heroines? Did you aspire to be like them?

Star Trek may no longer be aired in prime time on major networks, but with recent movies, the franchise is far from buried and forgotten. I certainly remember when the series' ideology held sway within our hearts and minds and influenced our future. We can probably credit *Star Trek* for inspiring our flip phones and computer tablets, among other things. Can we afford to bury the morality *Star Trek* taught us, or shall we revive it? So many of us yearned for a world akin to *Star Trek* – and not just for the cool gadgets! Can we remember when the values of Gene Roddenberry and the massive numbers of Trekkies showed the way and held the promise for the future?

What will it take for the collective consciousness of all Earthlings to embrace those values of caring and sharing, of justice and equality, of science and humanitarianism? In *Star Trek*, we defeated the Borg. How do Americans unplug from the "group think" and hive mentality of fear-mongering, discrimination, divisiveness, greed and fundamentalism?

Perhaps we just have to remember how we felt watching the crew of the Enterprise and why we held those women and men in such high esteem. Resistance is not futile. In fact, peaceful resistance is imperative!

Chapter 18

Goddess Notices

As I prepared to write a book on sacred sites of Goddess in Turkey and consider leading another tour to Anatolia, or "land of the nourishing Mothers," my mind returned to our last trip to a rural and out of the way place there called Pessinus. Pessinus was sacred in ancient times as a center dedicated to Cybele, though her temple remains hidden beneath the sands of time and is as yet undiscovered by contemporary archaeologists.

This telling of my time in Pessinus might all sound trivial, but I remember feelings of sacredness there presented in surprising ways. Although we didn't find Cybele's temple, I believe I *felt* her there. It seemed her essence was alive in the people and the energy of the place. Burned into my memory were the kids playing with their cows adorning their heads with costume jewelry, jumping upon their backs, talking to them or walking them down the main road, not much more than a mud pathway. It was obvious this was just a daily occurrence, this joyous and playful interaction with their cows. As a city girl, I marveled at seeing the cows responding to the kids, like my cat would when I play with her at home. There was a special relationship there between humans and beasts, calling to my mind the Goddess as Mistress of the Animals.

That was not the only thing I remember about walking down that muddy road in Pessinus. What caught my eye and became seared into my memory was this old crone sitting in her doorway. She silently watched the kids, the cows and our entourage looking for the essence of Cybele. The old woman was dressed in what we Westerners would call a costume, though I suspect it might have been her native dress. She wasn't there selling anything or trying to make herself visible in any fashion. There was something about her gaze. It grabbed me and seemed to follow me. Though it was years ago, it feels like it was yesterday. Don't laugh, but I felt as if she was a conduit to Goddess, or Goddess in human form, overseeing our pilgrimage. I had this sense that our visit was not going unnoticed.

Fast forward to a few years later, and it happened again.

My husband and I temporarily loaned a statue from our personal collection to the Goddess Temple and Cultural Center of Orange County in Irvine, California. On Saturday night, June 22, 2013, under the fullness of a supermoon, the newly installed, larger-than-life-sized statue of the Egyptian lion-headed Goddess, Sekhmet, was consecrated before the public. She was welcomed to her new temporary home by a packed house of women and men. High atop her four feet tall, pyramid-shaped base, Sekhmet dominated the room in regal splendor. It was hardly a surprise, during the instant of her unveiling, smoke alarms suddenly went off and lights began to flicker, leaving no doubt to all assembled she was definitely in the sanctuary! Simply put, we believe Sekhmet noticed our devotion and let us know she was in the building.

The evening was filled with music, singing, dancing, drumming and recitations to dispel the disinformation about her most well-known myth, a patriarchal myth perhaps designed to cause women to be feared, or women to fear their own power. Sekhmet, a solar deity known today to help women and men transform and empower themselves, is rising at a crucial time in our history. Have no doubt she is on the rise as people strive to find their strength, tenacity, passion, creativity, and courage – their sacred roar!

Some readers might not know me well yet, but I don't have these kinds of feelings often or casually. I'll admit, I tend to be more left-brained, leaning toward being more skeptical, and I question everything as I struggle for balance with my right brain. I don't allow myself flights of fancy. Pessinus, Turkey, however, felt more potent to me than a lot of places. That veil between past and present, Goddess and mortal, felt a little thinner. Certainly at the Goddess Temple of Orange County, Sekhmet was with us.

And finally, there was this third validation; Goddess notices.

Practically to the day I was notified John Hunt Publishing accepted my proposal for this book, my beloved husband had a heart attack. I rushed him to the emergency room of the hospital, and within the hour he was having surgery. In those surreal moments of confusion, fear, panic, shock and worry, I got on the phone and called the women in my circle of friends to enlist their prayers, and of course, I prayed too.

Roy came through the surgery fine, and that first night he was in the hospital, I went home to try to get a good night's sleep and prepare myself for the care giving that was ahead. I dreamed and, surprisingly, I remembered the dream.

I was in a large cavernous room full of women. The energy was chaotic, and their voices were garbled and loud. Then from nowhere, a woman, whose face I did not recognize, approached, and I knew her to be an Isian priestess. She put three coins in my hands. Not the metal variety, but the more ancient clay or terracotta type. On them were engraved images of Egyptian goddesses and gods. As I gazed upon them, the images became colorful and began to move. In my mind, I heard the words, "The Gods are activated," and I knew Goddess and the Divine Masculine, perhaps Thoth or Anubis, heard the prayers of the women in our community.

Again, I was reminded, the Great She hears our prayers, and I am sharing this with you so you have no doubt. She notices.

Chapter 19

Embracing The Other

I was recently interviewed on a radio program, and the host asked me if I might name one way my mother influenced my life. I immediately knew the answer to her question. Evelyn, my mother, taught me to fight for the underdog. She never verbalized it, but I think she felt like an underdog. She grew up in Louisiana in the 1940's. It was a time when women had little choice about the direction their lives would take. Evelyn had no protections like Roe v. Wade giving her choice in her reproductive life. Her mother was a janitor, and education for women was not a priority. Her world view consisted of getting married, keeping a roof over her head and her kids fed. I still remember her and my stepfather, too poor for a decent meal because selling vacuum cleaners door to door was not putting food on the table. We ate corn chips with some cheese spread for dinner. Sometimes my breakfast cereal did not come with milk, but water to moisten it. I can still vividly see my mother getting ready for work, "making her face," as she called putting on her makeup, and doing her hair, melting wax and putting it on her two front teeth to hide the rot because she couldn't afford a dentist. I came to love those bologna sandwiches with potato chips between the slices of bread. (Buying ham was out of the question!) I didn't know how poor we were; that seemed like a yummy treat!

Never having taken a class in Women's Studies and a product of the conservative South, I don't think Evelyn can name the cause for her circumstances. I can still hear her misplaced loyalty to her conservative Southern roots as my stepfather, a northerner from Iowa, would try to explain what was wrong with the rampant ignorance and racism in the South. Sexism, however, never came up. After all, women just had their role in society. Evelyn's life path was laid out and was not in question. It was normal for the times, but I doubt she was happy. I wonder if she felt happiness was something she could hope for. In hindsight, I believe she was satisfied surviving. I wonder how her life would have been different if she had the option to finish high school and go on to college or if she could make enough money to be independent and not to have to get married or fulfill society's expectations that women have children. So, yes, Evelyn instilled in me a desire to fight for the underdog, probably because she felt there was no one fighting for her.

She encouraged me to reach out to the lonely kids on the playground who were rejected by the popular kids. We shared what little we had with neighbors who had less than us. She told me to go out and get what I wanted in life because it would not come "knocking on my door." She tried her best with what she had to work with, which wasn't much materially or education-wise, but she had compassion and empathy, which I believe, made her very rich.

So it is no surprise, today I consider myself a social justice advocate. I fight for The Other because today, so many more of us are The Other. We are the ones with a boot on our neck – the boot of white, male, fundamentalist Christian men and their female counterparts who benefit from the oppression of others. Yes, this is the root of so much of the oppression and denigration, and it's not just oppression from the elites. Often it's poor, white, male, fundamentalist Christian men and their female handmaidens who play their part in this patriarchal scheme. And of course, it is not just the Christian men.

Naming this foe, calling out so many white men as our oppressors sounds radical or scary to some, especially coming from a white woman. They don't recognize white male privilege in our society because it has always been the norm. They don't recognize institutionalized sexism, misogyny, racism and homophobia because it's also always been the norm, taught at their dinner tables and spewed from the pulpits on Sunday. Poverty is a punishment from God, some say. Capitalism, the free market and rugged individualism cures it all, no matter there is no level playing field out there, and everyone doesn't have the ability to get into a good school or borrow $20,000 from their parents to start a company. It's survival of the fittest, forgetting the teachings of Jesus. If you need help, you're a taker, even though corporations get corporate welfare with our tax dollars every day, but helping human beings is becoming less and less a priority and politically incorrect.

Predator capitalism, injustice, inequality, voter suppression, human rights violations, poverty, destruction of the social safety net, infrastructure crumbling, environment being poisoned, militarism, income disparity at all-time high levels, children going to bed hungry, women being subjected to state sanctioned vaginal probes for exercising their constitutional rights – so what? We used to have a name for some of you, though it has gone out of fashion. WASPs. White Anglo-Saxon-Protestants. Google it.

So, you just keep up with your scrap-booking and NASCAR. Keep listening to Fox News and Rush Limbaugh so you're safely insulated in that cocoon of media-sanctioned callousness. Don't learn how your religion has devalued women and decimated cultures. Don't bother to worry yourself that sexism and racism is a sin. Don't explore how history has been rewritten. Those things don't touch you. You're comfortable. Why should you care? That suffering is the plight of The Other, those people not like you, the ones that don't really count, at the margins of society, who you deem valueless. Their suffering is their punishment for not being like you and playing by your rules and worshiping your God, or more accurately, your version of religious dogma written by men. Only more and more of us are becoming The Other: black and brown skinned people, immigrants, gays, non-Christians, the poor and elderly, workers and women, environmentalists.

Now imagine your life path suddenly takes an unexpected turn. What if suddenly you're The Other? Will you be sorry then you did not stand in solidarity with the unions for supporting worker rights against corporations as CEOs give workers less and less while they pay no taxes and become extraordinarily wealthy from human exploitation? Will you ever be sorry you did not care about our violent and male-dominated culture's domestic violence against women or women having to resort to back alley abortions? Will you regret not fighting for equal pay and reproductive rights for women so they might achieve independence? Will it take your water being poisoned from fracking or all our food becoming GMOs for you to care about environmentalism? Will you care when it's your daughter's life in danger but she cannot have an abortion because white Christian men have obliterated the separation between church and state with their ideology? Next time you go shopping, do you know, or care, that the cashier standing there works a 38 hour week rather than 40 so her employer does not have to pay her any benefits and that her wage is so low she has to get taxpayer-funded food stamps, but food stamps too are under attack by Republican men who would rather spend all our tax dollars on militarism and to further enrich corporations already making skyrocketing profits.

I could go on and on, but you either get it, or you don't. You either have empathy for the planet and humanity, or you think if they are not like you, they are not your concern. Why think outside your bubble? Why risk and rock the boat? What would your peers think? Shudder! You are either part of the problem by your ignorance or complicit in your comfort. There are none as blind as those who will not see, and you probably are not seeing the ground swell of The Other rising out of the ashes. Peaceful resistance and rebellion is afoot around the world. Women, workers, gays, immigrants, brown and black skinned people, the young and elderly, the poor, the environmentalist, all are weary. We are weary of that boot of injustice and exploitation on our neck, and we are calling out our oppressor. It is patriarchy. It is too often white, male-dominated, mostly Christian-fundamentalist authority who would continue to control the masses because the Bible tells them they are entitled. No wonder Republicans have to cheat to win elections. More and more people are getting a clue their policies benefit no one but the 1%.

Do you hear our sacred roar? We are coming armed with ideals of the Sacred Feminine. We are carrying with us the archetypes of not just Mary and Kwan Yin but Kali, the Morrighan, Libertas and Sekhmet. We're tired of waiting for you to evolve and do the right thing. No more will we tolerate a world of injustice and inequality. No more will we allow the destruction of Mother Earth. No more will be sit quietly and obediently as our dignity is stripped from us and our futures stolen. No more will our sexuality and reproductive rights be in the hands of religious zealots and their handmaidens. We want partnership. We want accountability. We want dignity and freedom. We want reverence for the earth and all of humanity. We want a world of compassion and empathy where we recognize our interconnection and practice caring and sharing for the 99%. There is enough for us all if it is equitably distributed.

And before you get the wrong idea, I don't hate Christians. I know too many good ones doing great work in the world. Myself, I'm a recovering Catholic, and I see the Divine Masculine in Jesus and believe in his message as he taught women and preached empathy, compassion and charity while rejecting greed and wealth. Goddess and God belong alongside each other. It's patriarchy who divorced the Sacred Feminine and Divine Masculine. And no, I'm not a lesbian, nor am I on welfare, as some white men have assumed when they read my posts on social media. Neither do I hate men or need sex as I've also been told by far too many white men on Facebook, ironically their own comments proving my point. I have been married to a wonderful man for over thirty years who is the wind beneath my wings. So call me feminist. Call me a Pagan. Call me politically incorrect or divisive. Call me a loud-mouthed and uppity woman. Call me radical, if you will, for shedding light and having the courage to name the root of our problems. Call me anything you like. I don't care. I'm not afraid, because of something else my mother taught me: *Sticks and stones will break my bones but words will never hurt me.*

Chapter 20

No Free Lunch – Building Community Has a Price

Growing into being a Goddess Advocate, I constantly heard about the need to build community and to have a temple, a physical space we could call our own. To some it would take the form of an outdoor space. Others wanted a brick and mortar building housing a school and healing center. And while some were against anything resembling organized religion, still we dreamed of buying an apartment complex or retreat center where the like-minded might live together and be supported by community. Desire aside, with the exception of temples like the Goddess Temple of Orange County that runs 24/7, and a handful of others across the country and globe, our dreams rarely manifested. So if religious faith is often the foundation for building a community, let's examine if there are clues as to why it might be particularly hard for Pagans to move beyond small covens, circles, living rooms and the annual Pagan Pride event to build thriving communities. Let's start by first looking at a list of what I call the Big Picture Challenges we face.

If religious faith *is* the foundation for community, what happens when we don't have a universal liturgy, creation myth or a sacred text that unifies and provides cohesion for our beliefs? I've heard people leaving Goddess Spirituality or Neo-Paganism because they thought it lacked substance or they couldn't recognize its relevance in today's world. Rarely do we take our myths and use them to teach values for living. So finding Paganism lacking, they instead gravitated toward religions or spiritualities providing more organization, structure, meaning, and rules beyond following a Wheel of the Year or the Wiccan Rede. They expressed their feeling that many of our groups do not teach much about what it means to be spiritual, how to have healthy boundaries or how to reflect upon whether we're acting ethically. Believe what you will about the Emperor Constantine, but when he, a Pagan most of his life, used Christianity as a glue to solidify the kingdom, he realized the importance of a common belief or thread to weave together disparate factions. And though most of us might hate religious dogma and value independent thinking, obviously it has its advantages over sectarian separatism.

Continuing along the lines of separatism, the mystery religion of Mithras, so popular in Imperial Rome, was quite the challenge to Christianity; however, one reason cited by some scholars for the religion not becoming more influential was women were excluded. When our goddess or pagan groups are segregated by gender, do we not run the same risk? Women-only groups take a particularly hard hit when you consider women still unfortunately make less money than men and therefore have less discretionary income, and it does cost money to build a viable community. So are women-only communities a recipe for failure? Consider a woman cannot include her husband or male children in her spirituality. Does that not call into question how deeply a woman can commit to the community; does that not also hurt the community's long term sustainability? And some might question if it's ethical, spiritual or wise to build a community based on what some see as sexist or discriminatory foundations.

I believe another major factor contributing to why we do not have larger communities is we do not use *fear to motivate* – no fire and brimstone and warnings of what might befall us if we are not baptized or accept a particular god as our savior. **So there's no penalty for not being Pagan**.

Next are our visibility issues. Where are the pagan soup kitchens and missionaries visibly doing good works in the community to elevate Paganism and share the wisdom within? With the exception of a mere handful of leaders on the national and world stage, where are the pied pipers extolling the benefits of Paganism and advocating for Goddess ideals and values as the answer to many of humanities woes? Yes, we are at the Parliament of World Religions now, and we've recently won a spot at the table at the American Academy of Religions, but why are there not more of us activated on the front lines fighting as Pagans for Gaia for religious tolerance, partnership, justice, peace, and human rights?

No doubt, it is because we have not yet won the battle of perceptions. Let us start by considering if our very labels need rehabilitation. The term Pagan is considered by many a term of derision used by Christians. It's a linguistic tool of persecution, a slanderous and a pejorative term for polytheists. Christian propaganda has similarly tainted the titles "witch" and "priestess", and this insidious propaganda continues to exist. It is hard for some to come out of the broom closet and tout our beliefs without fear of some retribution because the very term pagan has become so demonized or misunderstood in too many circles. Many of us do not or cannot use our own names publicly. We have to be careful not to have our photo taken at Pagan events, often with good cause. We all know that Christians have infiltrated all levels of government and public office. This often results in discrimination that sometimes makes getting 501c3 status, custody of children, housing, or even jobs more difficult if you are Pagan. When you consider these facts, no wonder we keep a low profile.

But being silent and not stepping up has its price too. It costs you in the allies you might never partner with, and it costs you the understanding you might never *seed*. I don't think I'm the only one who sees the religious intolerance toward Muslims and thinks that backlash could so easily turn on us if some unbalanced pagan did something stupid, and it got national attention. We lack much needed robust megaphones to control our own messaging and not let other faiths dictate who we are to the rest of the world.

Another element, a double-edged sword if you will, both positive and a hindrance, is our belief we do not need any intermediary to access the Divine, hence, less need perhaps for an organized career clergy. That can result in no one stepping up long term, 24/7, professionally, taking on the mantle of spiritual leader or visionary to advance the community. There is also the perception among non-pagans we have no clergy. Many pagan ministers have had difficulty ministering to the sick in hospitals or attract curious looks when presiding over handfastings, marriages or burials in public places.

Then there's money. My experience has been few pagans seem to understand the importance of reciprocity or believe in tithing or donating toward the growth of a community or temple, while other faiths require congregants donate a portion of their income to their church...

Which brings me back to our lack of physical brick and mortar temples, schools or healing centers. It's a Catch 22. If we are not visible in the community, if we do not appear to be in the legitimate business of religion with a center or place of worship on street corners, how can we expect to attract not just more congregants to carry out the work and pay the bills, but equally important, wealthy benefactors who might make healthy donations? If we are not perceived as credible and legitimate organizations, yes, even recognized by the government so that donors can receive tax deductions for their donations, then we also aren't eligible for all the help and tax benefits other religious groups enjoy. Just being associated with a recognized or traditional religious institution makes all the difference in so many practical ways, so we must realize the credibility bar for pagans is so much higher to clear.

The City University of New York did a poll that showed when the many hybrids of goddess-oriented or earth-based spiritualities were grouped together, it was one of the fastest growing groups in the United States. However, how many within these numbers actually take our faith seriously enough to make Goddess ideals integral to their everyday lives? And might there be some issues inherent to Pagan communities that never cause a problem in Christian churches, namely, the people curious about learning to manipulate energy and do magic? I hear complaints all the time that classes on sex magic, love spells or prosperity rituals are guaranteed to fill while classes on service, ethics, politics and herstory are less likely to draw students. Another problem I doubt Christian communities face is that younger people don't join the neighborhood Church for shock value or to rebel against authority. I also suspect people come to Goddess church, or rituals, to be entertained, not to do their spiritual work or learn a morality tale.

Taking this a step further, as Pagans, do we understand what it means to reconcile our spirituality with our politics and reflect those Goddess ideals in our choices, including in the voting booth? Do we believe it's important to have our values and beliefs recognized and our voices be a part of a larger national dialog? Do many Pagans realize Goddess ideals offer a road map for a sustainable future? **We have a lot to do in the way of providing a baseline for education among Pagans everywhere.**

Now let's take a look at what questions we might ask before building a local community:

First, we will have to define what we mean by community. Who is in the community? How wide are we casting the net? Will we include both genders? Progressive Christians? Environmentalists? How will you recruit members? Will you actively seek out angels or benefactors? Will you buy or rent meeting space? Can you pay for all the peripheral costs involved?

How will your presumably legal religious business be structured? Hierarchy? Partnership? Council? Dictatorship of a charismatic leader? Rotation of leadership? Consensus or majority rule? Will you be a religious or educational entity?

What is the mission, ethics and vision of the community? Will you have a school and seminary? What will you teach beyond Wicca 101? Is it important to try to provide childcare and elder care? Do you have enough reliable and capable people to handle the teaching, administration, and spiritual guidance? Will these people receive a salary? What is the responsibility of members? Will they be required to tithe, teach, volunteer, attend classes on history, ethics, partnership and how to do their spiritual work? Will there be an ethical and fair way to work out grievances among members? Will your community try to be active in the greater community?

Will you have professional, career clergy? What will be their responsibility to the community, and will they be monetarily compensated?

So there's a lot to think about. Some believe pagan communities are in their infancy. There are not yet sufficient numbers of us to accomplish building such thriving and service-oriented communities. But we are making progress. We must remember Christians started long ago meeting in living rooms much like many of us do. They did not always wield the power and influence we see in their hands today. In fact, we might remind ourselves, there were no doubt times when they wondered if their fledgling faith might survive at all.

And our numbers are growing. The idea of the Sacred Feminine is becoming more mainstream everyday creating possibilities for many partnerships. Women's issues, very much a part of the politics of Goddess Spirituality, is on the radar screen of governments and organizations across the globe and has been cited as the moral imperative of our time. Progressive Christians are helping us fight the fight for a feminine face of god in liturgy and churches.

If we want to build a community that grows beyond our individual broom closets, covens and annual Pagan Pride events, we must recognize there is a cost for this security and comfort, and Mother Nature provides the template. She shows us insuring a bountiful harvest to get us through both fat and lean times does not happen without work and a healthy respect and interdependence between human and Mother Earth. Nor does it happen without reciprocity. To grow a community, we must **plan** and **plant** and **tend** the **seeds** if we expect our garden to flourish. These seeds are our investments in the community and take the form of contributions by many in teaching, cooperation, thoughtfulness, tithing, energy and dedication. But first we must see if the land is fertile before we plant. We must ask if we have the right ingredients in the necessary amounts and the knowledgeable farmers to cultivate our community. Are we willing to grow up and move beyond "pagan time" and our infamous "herding cats" work ethic to move toward having a growing and sustainable community based on Goddess ideals?

These are just some of the considerations and questions we must ask ourselves and reflect on as we consider if the effort required will net a large enough return on our investment. One thing is for sure, there is no free lunch because building a community has its costs. Only time will tell if we are going to grow into a movement that will help save the world and make our Mother proud. Only time will tell if we will be the instruments of her sacred roar.

Part III

Meditations

Chapter 21

Sekhmet – Fires of Transformation

Find a comfortable spot to sit or lay down. Relax and breathe. Breathe deeply. In and out. In and out. Let the worries and cares of everyday life drift away. Try to focus on the sound of my voice.

You're laying down in a cool green meadow. Tall grasses are all around you. A line of trees are in the distance and behind that, tall mountains still with traces of winter snow at the highest peaks. You feel the cool, gentle breeze on your cheeks. You are perfectly relaxed. Comfortable. You are not worried or concerned about a single thing. The sun is shining brightly overhead and you are content, soaking in the beauty and abundance the Mother has provided.

As you lay there on your back, eyes shaded toward the sun, you hear a slight rustle in the tall green grasses just beyond you. There seems to be something moving closer toward you, but you are not alarmed. You are perfectly relaxed as you hear the gentle footsteps making their way toward you. You are in the domain of the Mother, and you know you are perfectly safe.

As the sound coming toward you stops, you look over in that direction, and partially cloaked by the grasses you see the outline of a large golden feline. What catches your attention are her eyes. She looks at you. Through you. In that instant you feel her energy like sunbeams projecting toward you making you feel powerful, capable, nurturing, and wise. As you continue to gaze into each other's eyes, you suddenly feel your surroundings go hazy and liquid. The big cat moves closer to you, inviting you toward her. Your eyes are inches apart from each other, and you covet this magnificent feeling she emanates in your presence. Within seconds you no longer see her, but you feel her. Inside you.

You look down at your feet, and they are shifting shape,

painlessly, miraculously, wonderfully. You look at your arms and hands, and they too are beginning to look like the supple, agile, limbs of a feline. You attempt to utter your astonishment, and your voice comes out in guttural purrs. Then you look to your right, and She is standing beside you. It is Sekhmet, the lion-headed Egyptian Goddess. You see her walking upright as a feline woman. She is beckoning you to walk alongside her. She takes you by the hand as you both walk together through the tall grasses. All the while you feel her eyes and breath on you. Her intense stare is imparting not only ancient wisdom, but courage, strength and tenacity as her gifts.

While you were basking in the glow of this energy, you had not realized she had walked you beyond the grasses toward a cool grotto of trees. You see a cave in the distance. She gestures for you to walk toward the cave. Behind you all the while, supporting you, silently imparting discernment and knowledge, she directs you to sit in the cool inviting darkness of this womb-like space. You hear her voice in the silence telling you to close your eyes. And in your mind's eye you see images, and these images impart sounds and give you a higher sense of awareness. Sit a few moments with these images and ideas. Let them flow to you. Absorb them as if you were a sponge. Remember the ancient wisdom you are being shown.

PAUSE.

You feel the images fading, getting harder to grasp, until they finally cease. They are like sand slipping through your fingers. You naturally open your new feline eyes, and you see clearly in the darkness. You breathe deeply, and as if by doing so, anchor in these new found ideas, thoughts, and messages. You no longer see her there physically, but you still feel the lingering energy of her presence within you. You feel your empowerment, your agility, and your creativity, and you flex these new-found muscles.

Soon, you know it is time to exit the cave. Walking toward the opening, you glimpse the sunlight just beyond. As you step into the full light of the golden sun, you glance down at your feet, hands and arms, and they are once again your own. You walk back through the tall grasses feeling the green growing things gently caressing your limbs as you go. But that is not all you feel. You feel changed and transformed.

You return to that sacred spot where this all began. You sit down on the soft, velvet-like grass and breathe. Breathe yourself back into awareness. You are relaxed, but you are also transformed for she is still and always will be a part of you.

Take a deep cleansing breath and slowly bring yourself back into this room. Open your eyes and breathe.

Chapter 22

Goddess of Spring - Potential Within/Interfaith

Find a comfortable position. Close your eyes and breathe. Breathe in and out. Breathe in and out. Allow your mind to release any thoughts as you make ready for our inner journey. Let the suggestions of the journey unfold on the movie screen of your third eye. Breathe in and out. Drop into that special space you go to to receive suggestions from the Divine. Allow. Allow. Allow. Be ready to open yourself to ideas and guidance important for you to grasp. Breathe. Allow. Allow yourself to be a container filling up with inspiration and wisdom you might glean from this journey. Let your consciousness go deeper, moving away from this place. It is as if you are sinking into luxurious pillows or walking down a flight of stairs. One step at a time. You go deeper and deeper with each step. Breathe and relax. Keep moving down that staircase to the potent darkness of your being.

Keeping your eyes closed, you allow the movie screen of your mind to switch on. And you see you have just transported to the most beautiful meadow. The sun is shining high in the bright blue sky, and you feel its warmth. You see flocks of birds overhead and hear their calls. The clouds are like fluffy wads of cotton in the heavens. Lowering your eyes, as you look around, you see a grove of trees before you. You hear the tap, tap of the red-headed woodpeckers on the ancient trunks. There are spatterings of flowers growing here and there: blue irises, yellow daffodils. You look down and see you are standing in a field of green clover. You notice some of the leaves have three leaves and others four. You feel truly lucky to be alive and embraced in Mother Nature's garden.

Then you realize you hear the rush of water behind you and feel a light spray of wetness. Turning around, you see a magnificent waterfall. You feel drawn to move toward the flowing water, being a creature of water that you are. As you walk toward the life-giving liquid, you see the other creatures that the water has also attracted. There are frogs and turtles making their way along the banks of the waterfall pool. Fish are abundant in the waters. Purple water lilies float upon the surface. There is even a timid young doe getting a drink. Then you notice playing in some high grasses just alongside the water's edge is a clutch of white rabbits. Some are nibbling the green blades of grass; others are taking care of their young ones. All are busy playing in Gaia's garden.

Moving closer to the waterfall, you notice there seems to be a path of stones that will take you behind the falling water. You sense the cool darkness there, and it calls to you. Stepping along the path, you reach out for a tree to steady you. As you do, you notice that the branches are filled with birds, and their joyful songs uplift your spirits even higher. Your keen eyes notice the many nests in the branches, and one nest, very close to you, holds several pale blue eggs. Soon the mother bird returns to tend this nest, and you continue along your stone path leading behind the waterfall. You are grateful for the glimpse of life you saw within the branches.

Soon you are behind the waterfall, and your eyes have to adjust to the darkness. You realize this cave behind the water's edge goes deep into the mountain. You feel perfectly at ease as you begin to go deeper within the cave. There is a peace and serenity in its coolness that lures you still deeper. Looking down, you notice some squirrels retrieving nuts they've hidden among the rocks. And the white rabbits you saw earlier are also here. They take no notice of you, so you decide to sit upon a large rock perfectly positioned to be a comfortable seat. Here you enjoy simply watching the rabbits and squirrels go about doing the things that they do.

Suddenly you see a white mist that seems to emanate from the rear of the deep chasm before you. The mist swirls and moves toward you and around you, piquing your curiosity. You wonder at your fearlessness but you feel secure in this womb-like space. Within seconds the mist seems to take a more solid shape, and you hear a voice. "Do not be afraid. I am here to teach you that which you seek."

Trusting and curious, you sit and wait for what might happen next. Within a few seconds the mist has taken the form of a beautiful woman who reaches out with her hand and touches the top of your head, gifting you with vision.

You see in this vision a woman on a throne, flanked by two lions. To her right is her consort on his throne. You see the consort's skin is a pale green like the flowering earth. From a large seed on his lap, you see vines and flowers growing forth. They entwine around his royal chair and encompass his body, becoming his clothing. Then, in what seems like time-lapsed photography, the green growth matures, growing larger, fuller and more abundant. The Divine Feminine tells you to look upon his face as it morphs from one face to another. Without knowing exactly how, you intuit that you are seeing the faces of the great old gods or consorts of Goddess: Tammuz, Osiris, Dionysus, Attis and Jesus, the flowering, dying, and rising kings. She smiles at you saying, "They are One."

The Spring Goddess touches your head again, and the scene changes. Your seat is now within a nest-like enclosure, and all around are colored eggs. You see red and blue, yellow and green eggs. Some have symbols on them: flowers, spirals, ankhs, crosses, wavy lines, interlocked triangles. She points to one egg, and you know you are meant to touch it. As you do, you hear the words, "Ah the Garden – there is wisdom and magic in all my creations!" You smile at Ostara in amazement. Yes, you know her by her name now. She is the Goddess of Spring.

She points to another egg, which you touch. Again you hear words of wisdom. "When I let go of who I am, I become who I might be." This makes you smile, and you exchange an understanding glance with Ostara, who points to a yellow egg just within reach. Again you hear her words, "Within you there is an inner seed of radiance waiting to grow." You are aglow with these truths and hopefulness. You then notice the mist that was Ostara is beginning to fade. Slowly, slowly you are alone once again in the dark womb of Gaia. But as you look down, there at your feet, there remains one red egg. You know this egg is yours to keep. As you reach down and touch it, you are gifted with one last seedling of truth that might grow within you. Sit a minute with the red egg, and let that wisdom enter your heart and mind.

PAUSE

If you haven't received the message yet, don't worry yourself. It will come. Take the red egg with you. Take it home, and put it upon your altar so that it is a constant reminder of the wonders of this journey and the potential of both Spring and the dark places.

You rise now and begin to exit the cave. You take one last look at the white rabbits as they frolic in the safety of the Mother's embrace. As you reach the stone pathway leading outside, the bright sunlight warms your skin once again, and you decide to sit for a moment at the bank of the pool. As you lower your feet into the waters so teeming with life, that sudden shock of cold transports you back here with us quickly and safely. When you are ready, you can open your eyes.

Enactment: You might consider setting up an altar, and on it put a basket of those plastic eggs that twist apart. Type or write on small slips of paper positive affirmations or qualities one might want to bring into their lives. Put the slips of paper in the eggs, and allow your group to take an egg that calls to them when they come out of the meditation.

Chapter 23

Tree Goddess – Pruning Your Divine Tree

You are sitting cross-legged in green meadow. You're breathing in the smell of freshly cut grass and breathing out stress and worry. You're breathing in sunshine and cool breezes and breathing out uncertainty and angst. Continue to breathe good things in. Things which no longer serve you are exhaled out.

As you breathe, you send your red cord down through your torso, and it begins to penetrate the Mother Earth. Breathing it down, down, down, it roots you to Gaia. As you breathe in, you breathe in her energy. She fills and renews you. As you breathe out, your cord becomes more deeply embedded in the body of our Great Earth Mother. In and out. In and out. You grow stronger with every breath of your sacred connection.

Now, keeping your eyes closed, you focus on the movie screen of your third eye. You see yourself seated in this green meadow, but you are surrounded by a circle of trees. The trees are of many different varieties. They have different types and colors of bark on their trunks. Their leaves are different sizes, colors and shapes. You hear the leaves rustle in the cool breeze.

You continue to breathe and watch the trees, when suddenly before your eyes, the trees begin to morph into the shapes of women – different women of different traditions. They are different sizes and shapes. They're dressed differently. You see the circle of tree-women glow a greenish-silver glow that pulses with each breath you take. You feel they are connected to you. You and they are one body, one breath.

Then suddenly you notice you are no longer seated cross-legged on the green meadow. Your red cord has morphed into tree roots, and you too have become a tree. As you're standing there, encircled by these tree-women, you relax into your new form, your new reality, because you know you are perfectly safe. You begin to intuit these tree women are speaking to you. You listen closely and focus, so you hear what they're telling you. You begin to understand they are Goddesses of the harvest, of the corn, of rice and fruit, of many varieties of green growing things. Now you recognize them. There is Demeter and Artemis, the Corn Mother, Ceres, and Pomona. Rice goddesses of Asia are here, too. They are all here, with many different faces, and they may be called by different names, but they are One. They are all aspects of the bountiful, fruitful Earth Mother, and you are a part of her.

The din of their voices subsides until you hear but one voice. She tells you to go within – to focus on the branches of your tree. She tells you that you must take stock. You must become aware of what branches need pruning. What must you cut away so that the rest may flourish?

You heed her words and begin to focus on your many arms which are branches filled with leaves, but then you notice some of the branches are dry and brittle. They are withered and no longer serve you. What do these branches represent in your life?

Bad habits? Toxic people? Fear? Uncertainty? Being mean-spirited? Having a tendency to gossip? Jealousy? Eating too much sugar? Being uncaring? Callous? Do these branches represent a lack of gratitude? What is it that prevents your tree from growing to new heights? What must you prune to become fuller, stronger and more rooted? Take a moment to think about this.

PAUSE

Allow, allow, allow these branches that no longer serve to fall to the earth. Sever them from your healthy branches. Return them to Gaia so they might become compost and help nourish the soil. Allow, allow, allow that which no longer serves you to depart and bid farewell. Sacrifice it to Mother Earth.

You understand you are stronger now. You have freed

yourself to flourish. You stand a bit taller having pruned the withered branches which offer no nourishment. You take a few moments to revel in your new stature – to feel the breeze blowing through your beautiful branches. You hear the rustling of your leaves. What a grand tree you are! Then you hear the Goddess Artemis tell you she was once worshiped as a tree, and you see her smile at you.

You look up into the sun on the movie screen of your third eye, and its glow casts a bright light over you and the ring of Goddesses surrounding you. In a few moments, the glow slowly fades, as does their circle. You realize you are standing alone once again in the green meadow. You are no longer a tree. You are you, but a stronger, healthier you, more able to go forth and bear many fruit from your metaphorical branches. You know you can come back to this meadow. You can prune your divine tree anytime you must cut away that which no longer serves you.

Now slowly, come back to our sacred space. Open your eyes when it feels comfortable. Shake your hands. Make circles with your ankles. Take a final deep breath and bask in the glow of your communion with the Goddesses of the Harvest.

Chapter 24

Fortuna – Sacred Sanctuary of Manifestation

We are going to take a guided inner journey – a sacred pilgrimage to our inner landscape. Our goal is to allow each of you to discover and become acquainted with your personal sacred sanctuary. It's a place you can go for pleasure, for transformation, to solicit answers or to connect with the Divine Source or Goddess. You might find peace there in times of turmoil. Many people find a place in Nature and return to it as needed for comfort in hard times.

I'm going to invite you to relax. Find a position that's comfortable for you for the next few minutes. Turn off any cell phones. Let any stray thoughts that aren't related to what we're doing go for now. Let's settle in and begin to drop down into that special place you might already know the path to – or maybe this is your first time down a new path. Just trust in the exercise.

Let's close our eyes and breathe together. Take a deep breath in. Really expel it. Take another breath in and out. If you feel there's still stuff in there that needs to be purged, don't hesitate to take another cleansing breath to expel any anxiety or discomfort or thoughts that don't contribute to reaching our destination. Take your time. There is no rush.

Breathe in. Out. Breathe in. Out. I invite you to try to focus on my voice during this meditation. Try to stay with me. Cast off any random thoughts that might enter in and don't belong. But most of all, this experience is for you, so if you find yourself led on your own journey, that's fine.

Now I want you to begin to bring your focus to your forehead – your mind's eye or third eye. However you refer to it, think of it as a movie screen where you'll see a visual account of this guided journey. Give yourself permission to feel perfectly comfortable, embracing the elements we encounter on our trip. Give yourself permission to allow, allow, allow the ideas and images that come to you. Let the spigot flow. Later you can decide what to keep and store away or discard.

Our journey begins on a cobblestone street. You are alone except for the call of birds overhead. You're barefoot and feel the coolness of the stones beneath your feet. You savor the nourishing sunshine and breeze on your cheeks. A short distance away, you notice a door that grabs your attention. You like the lion's head door knocker, and you walk closer for a better look. You walk closer and closer. You're completely comfortable and curious. As you touch the door knob of the wooden door, it seems to slowly begin to dissolve, or perhaps you can see through it. Beyond the door, you see a natural place of beauty, and you walk through.

What does that look like to you? This is a very personal sacred sanctuary all your own. Perhaps beyond there's a temple or a grove of old trees or a lake. Let yourself see this place perfectly suited just for you. Take a few moments and let the vision manifest.

What's the light like? The temperature? Are you standing in grass or sand? Give yourself a moment to soak in this landscape so a picture of this place lives on the canvas of your mind.

You walk forward into this very sacred and personal place that is all your own. Before you've gone very far, you see before you the outline of a woman in the distance. Can you see her? Let your eyes linger on her appearance. Is she wearing a crown? A cloak? Does she remind you of a particular woman? Maybe a Goddess?

The woman beckons you toward her, and you find yourself standing just before her, only an arms length away. She smiles at you, and you are completely comfortable. Take a moment to feel what emotions come up for you being here with this woman.

PAUSE

In a moment you hear her voice speaking to you, though her lips seem not to be moving. You realize she is communicating with you telepathically. She asks you your name, and you answer. She tells you that you have discovered a very special place – a place that you alone have been gifted entrance. Then she points to the cornucopia she holds in the crook of her arm. You see it is filled to overflowing with various fruit. She bids you to take a red fruit from the cornucopia and bite into it. As you do you are suddenly filled with a knowing. You have an answer to something you have been seeking.

Take a minute and check in. How does that make you feel? What knowledge was imparted to you just then?

PAUSE

Then you hear the woman speaking to you again. She asks what it is you have come to discover. What is it you're longing for? What is it you really want? You take a moment or two to think about the answer to this question.

PAUSE

Then as you tell her what it is you seek, what you really want, she reaches out her hand and lays it upon your head. You feel comforted by her touch, and you start to notice a warmth within your body, starting from her touch and moving down your spine and limbs to your toes. You hear her voice telling you to see that which you seek manifested.

Visualize yourself possessing that which you desire. Feel it happening. See your life with everything perfectly in place. You take a moment to do as she commands. Allow, allow, allow. Take a moment to see. Let this shift, this new reality, become a part of you. You let go of any resistance and align yourself with your desires. You no longer see obstacles. You see only possibilities and potential.

PAUSE

As you look at the woman, you notice there is now a transparency about her. A golden aura or glow silhouettes her body. You see she is holding a small box. She lifts the box toward you and opens the lid. Within is a key, and she gestures for you to take it. She tells you this is the key to your personal sacred Sanctuary of Manifestation. You may come here as needed to enable you to seek the answers you desire. You need only remember this meeting and feel the key in your hands to access this special place at will. You may come here to find what it is you need. This is your place of imagining and transformation.

You look down at the key, then look back up at Fortuna holding her cornucopia, but she has suddenly become mist, and she is fading, becoming dimmer and dimmer. Before she totally dissolves, you hear her voice saying one last thing: "You are loved. You are empowered. You are my sacred creation. Have no fears my child. You have found the path to Source. All will be as you need."

With the last vestige of her apparition gone, you feel a sudden breeze. You find yourself back on that cobblestone street. You hear the birds overhead andfeel the wind on your cheeks. You take a deep breath and remember Fortuna and your sacred Sanctuary of Manifestation. You feel the invisible key in the palm of your hand to unlock this place for future visits. You know you may come back when you have the need.

Now slowly, allow, allow, allow yourself to return to this room in the time that is comfortable for you. Take a deep breath. Wiggle your feet and hands and toes. Say your name out loud. Stand up and move around. Shake off the feelings of being on that inner landscape.

Chapter 25

Kwan Yin – Healing

Relax and breathe, keeping your eyes closed. Let the stress and worries of the outside world fade away. They have no place in this room. If your mind wanders, let it just come back to the sound of my voice. See the images I suggest on the movie screen of your third eye. Breathe. Breathe. Allow yourself to go to that place within, that place that holds the wisdom, that place that connects to the Source, and that place from where your connection to all life comes forth and grows. Breathe. Breathe. Keeping your eyes closed, focus on the sound of my voice, and let it be your guide.

You see yourself on a sunny beach. The sand under your skin is warm and shifts under your body with each motion. You hear the tide from the ocean very near rolling in and out, with its ebb and flow. Ebb and flow. The sound has you mesmerized as you allow yourself to lie there soaking in the peacefulness of this quiet place. You feel drawn in and notice your breath has become one with the ocean tides, in and out, in and out. You feel as if you are about to doze off when you hear a sweet melody in the distance. It piques your curiosity. You wonder where this sound might be coming from because you thought you were alone in this far-away place. You decide to get up and explore. You gather yourself from this place on the beach and walk toward the sand dunes rising high behind you. As you climb to the top of the dunes and look between the tall grasses, you can see in the distance a large natural opening in the rocky cliff. You listen to the melody and are intrigued. You walk closer to the cave entrance. What possibly might be within making this beautiful, ethereal sound, coaxing you forward, tempting you within.

In a moment or two, you are standing at the entrance to the

cave. You feel the coolness within compared to the warmth of the sun's rays on the beach. The darkness is inviting, and you feel drawn to go within. You feel no sense of danger, only a strange sense of calm, so you allow yourself to go deeper within. You are surprised how your eyes acclimate to the darkness, allowing you to see with ease. It's almost as if there is some natural light that reflects off the shimmering stones you see protruding from the rocks that permeate the cave's interior. The melody continues to invite you within, so you walk deeper, all the while mesmerized by the beauty of this darkness and the sensation that something lies deep within you must see.

As you go still deeper, you have no fear about being able to find your way out. The path has been easy, and the return leaves no doubt. You focus on the melody, and you are unsure if it is the voice of a woman or the strands of some ethereal instrument. You only know it has you within its sweet embrace. Interestingly, it seems, with each gust of breeze that emanates from within, the sound seems louder, as if the sound is carried on the breath of this place —as if this very cavern is alive. Intrigued and trusting your instincts, you go farther still within the cool and inviting darkness. There is no danger in this place. You must find the source of this enchanting sound.

In a moment you come upon a larger opening as the cavern becomes brighter, larger, and rounder. You notice a glint of something shining on the wall before you, and your eyes strain to focus. As you move closer, you reach out your hand and touch the golden source that seems encrusted in the rock. Instantly you jump back as the golden object begins to morph. You can hardly believe the transformation happening before your eyes. You stand there spellbound, unable to move, yet you are not afraid. The glint of gold is changing shape and growing and taking form. It is as if you have awakened something from its slumber. You are reminded of unbelievable stories from ancient myths – of seekers, sailors and travelers who chance upon the unexplained.

And here you find yourself a player in just such a wondrous story, and you choose to let your mind suspend disbelief. Mesmerized, you stand there and watch the full transformation as the glint of what appeared to be gold slowly materializes in a haze-like mist to reveal the body of a woman clad in shimmering robes.

How does she look to you? What color is her hair? What does she wear upon her head? Her feet? Can you see what she holds in her hand? It appears to be a jar made of the precious stone called alabaster. Your eyes are drawn to the jar and the gentleness of her hands and eyes. She seems to be speaking to you yet her lips do not move. You realize the melody you had been hearing is now becoming clearer, distant and alluring but without actual words you could understand. You now suddenly realize the melody is actually her voice, and you are slowly coming to understand the language that lives within the magical sounds emanating from her very being.

Transfixed on her golden form, you look closer, listening and trying to take in every detail because you know this experience is a very special gift. You let your eyes gaze upon her from head to toe. You see her golden form begin to glow, and the shimmer begins to spread toward you, as if you are magically being embraced in her golden essence. You feel its warmth, and you breathe deeply on instinct, soaking in that which is being given to you. You begin to realize this Great Mother is healing you of that which has tormented you. You feel that which gave you angst, pain, worry, fear and dread subsiding. As this revelation becomes more real, you seem to be guided to focus on that which was broken when you entered the cave. Perhaps your wounds were obvious. Perhaps not. But you are being shown in the presence of this Goddess you have the ability to overcome and heal.

In that moment, still in her golden embrace, you notice her fingers are reaching within the alabaster jar. Then she touches you to anoint your forehead. Her words until now had been a soothing, healing melody, but now they clearly take shape as she says, "I heal thee, my child, with this sacred salve. Never doubt your wounds can be healed. Never doubt the love I have in my heart for you, for I have created you and wish you joy and happiness. Go forth now. Live your life to its fullest. Follow your dreams. And remember I am always here for you."

As you take in her words, look again at this golden Goddess. What do you see? How do you feel here in her presence? Savor this moment and burn it into your memory. Allow the sensations of the moment to overtake you. Bask in her golden glow. Close your eyes and take in the healing and love she offers you. Feel it to your very core. Breathe it in and listen. Close your eyes and hear if there are any other words or messages she offers.

PAUSE

You notice that the golden glow that embraced you is beginning to fade. It is receding back toward the golden form of the Great She. You still feel her smile upon you. You feel her essence, but her shape is becoming faint and formless. Within a few minutes there is only the golden glint embedded within the rocks, and her voice is once again the natural melody on the wind that lives within this womb-like cavern.

You understand your audience has come to an end. But you know this is a place you can return anytime you need her golden touch, her loving embrace, her healing and guidance.

You turn around and begin to retrace your steps back toward the mouth of the cave. You breathe in deeply, remembering the faint melody that once called you with such urgency. You understand that she knew you needed her, and so she revealed herself to you. You reawakened her in your time of need, in your time of seeking, in your time of doubt.

Soon you see the rays of the bright sunshine before you. Once again the only sounds you hear are the ebb and flow of the ocean beyond. You step out into the brightness of day, and you are awakened.

You are back here in this room, where your journey began. Open your eyes and shake your hands. Say your name out loud. Bring yourself back from the sacred journey, refreshed, invigorated, and confident in your ability to call upon the essence you experienced in these past moments whenever the need arises.

Chapter 26

Isis – Temple of Ancient Wisdom

You are walking down the steps of the boat dock. Down, down, down this flight of stairs. With each step you allow yourself to go deeper within. With each step you breathe and connect to that sacred self within. You recognize the sparks of divinity within your sacred core. You climb aboard your golden barge, and soon your journey to the Temple of Isis is underway. As you travel along the waters of the Nile, you see the green papyrus growing on the river banks. You gaze at the white egrets in their gentle majesty, and you smile as you see the children playing in the shallow waters with the family water buffalo. Feel the gentle rocking of the boat. Feel the lapping of the waves beneath you. Allow, allow, allow yourself to go ever deeper within. Soon you are at the Temple of Isis, the destination of your long-awaited journey.

As you embark from your felucca, the traditional sailboat of Egypt, you can hardly contain your excitement. Exhilaration and awe flow through your body like a wave as you stand under the hot sun in the outer courtyard of this ancient stone temple. You take in the grandeur standing before you, and as if touched by the hand of the Lady of Mystery and Magic, you are amazed that you can actually decipher the hieroglyphic carvings in this revered domain of Isis. Here is one of the last Pagan temples to close under the pressure of the spread of Christianity. You run your fingers along the carvings and comprehend the inscriptions and images of this temple associated with Isis, She of Ten Thousand Names. Here this mighty Goddess stood on the fringes of the empire as a beloved protectress of its people.

Moving within the dark recesses of the temple, you begin to intuitively sense that taking a journey to this temple might suggest cultivating the ability to call upon the courage and strength of your own inner warrior or heroine. You know this means transcending the powerful and primal feelings of fear and anxiety that sometimes grips you and creeps with cold fingers up your spine. To teach yourself to master fear and access your personal empowerment, you instinctively seek out the cella, or holy of holies within this sacred stone fortress.

One turn down the hallway, and you find the heart of the temple. See it is lit only by the flames of a fire blazing in the copper cauldron within. Feel the intense heat on your skin. Suddenly you intuit you can cast your doubts and fears upon this sacred blaze, and by a sacred alchemy found only here, these unhelpful emotions morph within the heat and transform. In the flames, you can dissolve what no longer serves you and change the energy of these discarded doubts and fears into passion and strength that steel you and give you confidence, purpose and determination.

As you work with the alchemical energies, you will yourself to shift anxiety and angst into courage, fortitude and serenity. Here you are the shaman of the temple, able to wield the powers of transformation at will.

Suddenly, the walls of the cella surrounding you seem to go liquid. Your ears are filled with the sound of the heartbeat of the cella. You feel a pressure upon your temples and sense these powers begin to reverberate within every fiber of your being, until finally, a feeling of warmth swirls and settles in your torso. You understand you are receiving the gifts of Isis as they pour forth from the heart of the temple to fill you. You know you have now tapped into this reservoir of ancient power. You are filled with a knowing you can readily activate this essence anytime you must channel doubt and anxiety into energy to achieve your heart's desire.

Your work completed for now, you reluctantly leave the cella, but you turn back for a parting glance. You notice the cauldron of transformation has disappeared; before your eyes is a Milky Way of stars that contains the face of Isis. As you focus on this Cosmic Mother, rays of celestial light reach out toward you, and you understand her gifts were not limited to helping you access your inner strength and courage. They also want you to be aware of an important truth. As you look into her eyes, she imparts the wisdom that strength and courage are not always about wielding the biggest club or having the loudest voice. Strength and courage also manifest in many more subtle ways. They may manifest as gentleness or compassion as well as assertiveness or standing in one's own power in the face of adversity. It might mean applying discernment to resist recklessness. It could mean finding the cunning to know when to remain silent and wait as the energies of the Universe percolate.

As you exit the temple under the heat of the Egyptian sun and return to your felucca, a quiet calm seems to have permeated your psyche, and you silently thank Isis for these gifts of wisdom she has bestowed upon you in this sacred place. You feel wrapped in the golden embrace of the magical wings of Isis and know the many layers of strength that can be accessed here. All the way home, you contemplate what has just transpired and the wondrous journey you have just made.

Your felucca has now returned you to your dock, and you are back where you started. When you are ready, open your eyes, shake your hands and feet and bring yourself back into the room.

Chapter 27

Sleeping Goddess of Malta – Dreaming and Inspiration

Make yourself comfortable. Focus your attention on your third eye. Breathe in and out. In and out. Let the distractions of the mundane world drop away. They are not important now. Prepare yourself for a sacred journey. Allow, allow, allow peace and serenity to drop over you like a veil.

So you have finally arrived in Malta. You have come here to continue your quest to seek out life's mysteries and what they hold in store for you. No grand cathedral or elaborate structure holds the keys for you this journey. Instead you choose to explore these small islands hardly discernible on a map. No matter though, for as long as you can remember, you have been drawn to make this pilgrimage. Now here, the hair on the back of your neck is standing tall, and you can barely contain the rush of adrenalin shooting through your limbs. The ancient stone temples, shaped in the form of mother and daughter, have been unceasingly calling to you.

Now as you actually stand on the sacred landscape, you hear their call ever-more loudly as their voices blend and call out like sirens of old. Their silent lure, heard only in your heart and mind, conjures vague memories of a time long past when you may have been a priestess here in a past life. Perhaps you once performed sacred rituals within the womb of these structure of the Sacred Feminine, teaching about the mysteries, which seem just beyond your grasp in this life. Yet the connection between you and these oldest standing temples is still discernible. Now that you are actually here, that sacred cord connecting you and this place pulses with a new vibrancy, even if the images of the past had been but hazy blurs in your deepest dreams. You have felt driven and yearned to experience once again the intimate darkness and energy within the womb of the Mother, known as the Hypogeum. It is here the Sleeping Goddess of Malta was found, and you suspect it is her voice that has been calling to your subconscious mind.

Having left the impeccably clean cobblestone streets, with row upon row of whitewashed stucco houses, each adorned with their unique and ornate door knockers, you are finally here once again. You hesitate for a moment and take a deep breath in contemplation before entering within this much anticipated and long-awaited underground space because you understand the profound significance. You are about to cross the threshold between mundane and sacred, past and present, conscious and subconscious, and enter within the holy body of Gaia, or Mother Earth.

Casting anxiety aside, you are unable to wait any longer, and you step into another world. Inside, walking in the dim light, you can see the walls surrounding you, and you remember just beyond and below are sacred chambers that hold a memory of a time past that is yet to blossom again into its full potential. You relax in the cool, peaceful, stillness, and suddenly you have the sensation that you are an embryo gestating within a living womb. Your life and all its possibilities are still before you. As you open your mouth to give voice to your bliss, you are startled to hear its tone within the sacred labyrinthine chamber. You hardly recognize the magical qualities of its sweet song. Barely having comprehended this magical delight, you suddenly are distracted by a mist that appears from the darkness of a recessed niche within the chamber.

As you watch in awe, the mist takes the shape of the Sleeping Goddess upon her altar. Her body seems to expand and contract as she lies in silent slumber. As you stand there mesmerized, you notice her form is shimmering with a silver hue that seems to transmit thought. Wide eyed and amazed, you realize she is communicating with you to help and guide you. As your minds touch, you recognize her and know with certainty it has been her trying to reach you through your dream time. With every breath, she instructs you to go deeply within yourself to that vast limitless container residing at your core. She wants you to reflect upon the ideas and vision that live there and to acknowledge that which inspires you. You must have faith in your ideas and aspirations. She assures you that despite this time of uncertainty, when your life path may not be clear, you must trust in your divine guidance and gifts.

You recognize now, when you hear her calling or see the Sleeping Goddess, you are being reminded you have been going astray and are out of sync with your destiny and true purpose. Seeing her is a sign to listen to the guidance of your dreams. You are to seek your muse, guideposts, or inner healing by allowing yourself to hear the revelations born in the knowledge that incubates in your deepest self. Listen and trust your divinity within. Be willing to hear your own intuitive voice.

Having come so far to make this journey, you now know that when you feel lost or empty, you can always return here in your mind. Just breathe deeply and go within to the womb of the Hypogeum for a refill or to reconnect and hear the ancient voices of wisdom emanating there. Allow the shimmering silver radiance of the Sleeping Goddess to envelope you and help you find your way.

As you exit the Hypogeum, you put your hands together in a gesture of prayer and bow your head in thanks to the Sleeping Goddess for her awakening you to your dreams.

When you are ready, open your eyes, and shake your hands and feet. Speak your name aloud and return to this sacred space.

Chapter 28

Aphrodite – True Beauty and Self Worth

Find a comfortable place to sit and relax. Start to go within. Let the cares and worries of the outside world drift away. Breathe in and out. Breathe in and out. If you are having difficulty letting go of negative stuff, expel it from your body by breathing it out sharply. Do it again if necessary. Don't worry about the sound or be self-conscious. Focus on the core of your sacred self where the sparks of your divinity live. Breathe in and out. In and out. Prepare yourself for your sacred journey.

In coming to Turkey, or Anatolia, the land of the nourishing mother, you have come a long way to learn the full measure of who Aphrodite truly is, and perhaps who you are. Here in Aphrodiasias, where Aphrodite was revered in her full, potent, and magnificent splendor, the true nature of this Goddess is revealed, and in your seeking, dear pilgrim, you will certainly be rewarded.

So then, let us delay no longer, and imagine yourself standing before the temple of Aphrodite in her valley of Aphrodiasias. This was a town of artisans dedicated to memorializing in stone the authentic nature of Aphrodite. You can still hear the sound of chisel on stone coming from the artists' workshops lining the streets and hear the teachers instructing their pupils on their technique. Walking toward her temple, now standing on her sacred landscape, let yourself open to the essence of this place and feel what a fertile container for her devotion this once was in ancient times.

As the sun beats down upon your neck, you hear the call of the birds above and the singing of the babbling stream alongside the temple. Allow, allow, allow the mountains on either side to embrace you as if they were the arms of the Mother herself.

Allow, allow, allow yourself to expand your awareness and open to the true beauty and vast essence of this great Goddess. As you sit before the remains of her temple on the cool, green grass, you allow the image of Aphrodite created here to fill the movie screen of your mind's eye, and her essence envelopes your body, mind and soul.

In doing so, you see yourself differently. You look beyond the surface and begin to see what others, and yourself, may have yet to discover about you. Looking again at her statue, you begin to soak in the full extent of who this Goddess of Life and Death truly was. Not merely a Goddess called upon in matters of beauty or the heart, although that in itself was not a frivolous and superficial desire, here Aphrodite was that and more.

Lie down now upon the hallowed ground of her temple. Dig your fingers into the dirt. Pick a red poppy, her sacred flower, and put it in your hair. Imagine what it must have been like to have a large part of the world only see half of who she truly was. Drink her in. Try to know her and let her become a part of you. As you do so, you see the sacred within. You begin to recognize the seeds lying dormant within yourself which you can awaken at will. See the polos on her head, signifying her as the protectress of the people, and the registers of animals on her torso, naming her Mistress of the Beasts. It is she who provides all that one needs to sustain oneself. Let us know her for who she truly is in all her beauty and for all the treasures and worth she embodies, not just the superficial persona most attribute to her.

Perhaps this journey has triggered feelings within you as you seek to know who you truly are in this lifetime and determine your own self-worth. Here in this holy place, Aphrodite's image, embodied in her statue, reflects more accurately her full power and essence. She represented all there is from womb to tomb and then rebirth. Here she could truly be herself, and her more ancient roots and attributes were in full view for all the world to see, leaving no doubt about the extent of her abilities and power.

Here she embodies Cybele, Magna Mater and Mother Mountain. She is the Creatrix and sustainer of all life, and it is unto Her one returns upon his or her death.

Coming here means this archetype of Aphrodite is calling you to a higher awareness: to know your full measure and to claim your true beauty and self-worth. She is encouraging you to strive to honor yourself and know your value beyond mere reputation or what might show on the surface. She wants you to look deeply for what lies beneath and seek the true measure of yourself or perhaps that of another. Treasure is rarely found lying scattered upon the ground. Do not be misguided by "fool's gold" or false representations that openly glint in the sunlight. One must sometimes take the time to dig deep, uncovering the layers that may hide the treasure of one's true beauty, love and worth. Once found, wear your gifts with pride and self-assurance, like a necklace of pearls upon your neck. Allow, allow, allow your true beauty and self-worth to be known to all who cast their eyes upon your form and deeds.

As you parallel your new sense of self with that of discovering the truth of Aphrodite, realize there is much within you yet to blossom. With this new found truth, you feel your body glow. Aphrodite herself is activating the shakti within you. You feel the heat of awareness from the tips of your toes, up your spine, to the top of your head, and you know you are the catalyst, the activator, the spark, of your own becoming.

Now, with these mysteries revealed to you, bask in the glow of your authentic self, and before you leave this sacred space, quietly collect water from the sacred spring alongside the temple and place a red poppy upon the sacred stones of Aphrodite's temple.

When you are ready, open your eyes and return to this sacred place. Restore your senses to this world by shaking your hands and rotating your ankles. Perhaps get up, have a glass of water and bite to eat.

Chapter 29

Minerva – Sacred Waters of Wisdom

Find a comfortable position and relax. You are about to take an inner sacred journey. Ready yourself by breathing in positive thoughts and breathing out anything toxic. Breathe in focus and intention. Breathe out distraction and discontent. Breathe in confidence and healing. Breathe out self-doubt and dis-ease. Connect with that part of yourself that allows you to feel your divine spark. Allow, allow, allow the veil between your conscious and unconscious mind to drop. Allow, allow, allow that wall to dissolve.

The anticipation has been bittersweet, and you can hardly wait a moment longer. You have been waiting a long time to make this journey and have come from far away, but you have finally arrived! You breathe a sigh of relief as you gather your bathing attire and dressing gown and make your way toward the thermal waters. As you look at the inscriptions on display of patrons from ancient times, you allow your mind to wander to the distant past and wonder how much more difficult it must have been for pilgrims in those earlier times who had no luxuries of contemporary transportation as they journeyed to these sacred places of healing to take the cure.

You almost want to pinch yourself. You can hardly believe you will soon be immersed in the sacred thermal waters of Bath in England.

Walking within the hallowed halls, you look around and admire the confines of Minerva's temple and healing pool, and you visually soak in the delicate Roman archways and warmth of the stones that surround the sanctuary into which you are about to emerge. You see the various cool and hot pools you will no doubt partake of during your stay here. You are intrigued when you see these sacred waters are a golden color as they emerge from the earth.

As you approach your healing pool, the attendants speak in quiet whispers and help prepare you so that you might bathe alone in the comfort of the secluded, golden sacred waters. They light the sacred herbs to cleanse and purify your body and mind and encourage you to breathe in the healing smoke. As you do, you feel your body all aglow, tingling sensations tickling your fingers, toes and the back of your neck. After the appropriate prayers, you are now completely relaxed. You take a deep breath and remember feeling as if you are a brand new sponge about to absorb all Goddess has to offer you.

After a few minutes of relaxation and contemplation, you look up and notice you will be bathing under the watchful eye of the Celtic Goddess, Sul, and the Roman Goddess, Minerva, whose images you see overlooking the sanctuary. Under the bright sun, the time has finally come. You are ready to dip your first toe into the waters. You imagine the soothing warmth as a catalyst triggering your own innate wisdom to flow from that repository deep within you. Instinctively, you close your eyes and breathe. You lower yourself until your body is completely covered in the healing waters. The sensations flood you. You are relieved, peaceful and satisfied. It is as if Sul or Minerva have reached out and touched you, relieving you of all that ails you.

As you linger in the sacred waters, your senses are heightened. You feel and listen with every fiber of your being. Immersed to your neck in these warm healing waters, meditation is so much easier. The connection to Goddess comes more intensely and without so much effort – perhaps because we are creatures of water – perhaps because you are here in her sacred domain which has been a repository of her power. You feel her healing gifts bubble up to the surface of your psyche, and you receive the guidance relevant to sooth the wounds of your particular body, mind and heart.

You cast your eyes once again in her direction. Looking into the eyes of Minerva, you feel her wisdom to provide just the healing you need. You allow yourself to see your situation with a discerning eye and seek the antidote to what ails you. Perhaps you must forgive, compromise or commit. It may be necessary to ask assistance or go it alone. Make a decision, then take the steps necessary toward healing. Trust in the wisdom of your deep self. You know what to do. Somehow everything seems so much clearer now that you have been cleansed, purified and healed in the sacred waters of the Mother. The time for action has come.

It is hard to know how much time has gone by, but you feel you have received that which you needed. As you exit the pools, filled with gratitude for the healing and insight, you can leave with the wisdom and security of knowing you may always come here again should the healing waters of Sulis Minerva be a necessary salve for future ills.

When you are ready, return to us here in the room that was the origin of your journey. Open your eyes slowly, allowing the mundane world to creep back into your reality. Take a few breaths and come back now. Shake your hands, roll your ankles and speak your name out loud.

Chapter 30

Mary Magdalene – Unity and Wholeness

Ready yourself by finding a comfortable position from which to take your sacred journey. Breathe in and out. Ground yourself allowing your red cord to travel down your torso and legs and feet and anchor into Mother Earth. Breathe in. Breathe Out. Let the cares and worries of everyday life fall away. They are not important now. The only thing that is important is your connection to your divine spark within that will assist you in this journey. Breathe in and out. Let go, let go, let go of everything in the mundane world in these sacred moments.

As you stand on the steps of La Madeleine, the massive entrance doors before you, the noise of midday Parisian traffic and pedestrians a distant backdrop, you contemplate how long Mary Magdalene had been erroneously cast in the role of the prostitute. Yet here in the middle of Paris, Napoleon, on behalf of his soldiers, has built a temple in her honor, as if perhaps, righting a wrong that was so long in coming. Walking across the threshold of this holy place, opening the huge doors to her shrine, you wonder how Mary must have felt being so misrepresented and misunderstood for centuries. You imagine her disappointment and inner turmoil brought about by man-made dogma, and a sadness falls over you like a veil. The Beloved of Christ, relegated to insult and shame for so long, became the subject of disinformation that has thwarted wholeness and harmony for thousands of years.

As your eyes adjust to the low light within the temple, you instantly feel dwarfed by the immense size of this cavernous shrine. Your eyes are instantly drawn to the primary light coming from the altar at the front of the church. Absent are the typical patriarchal symbols of male authority. Instead you see

Mary in all her splendor, ascending to heaven, accompanied by angels, as she must anxiously await rejoining her beloved, Jesus. This scene triggers sweet memories of your own life as you contemplate the bliss of being joined with your own beloved, and the warmth of this remembering covers you like a comfortable blanket. Raising your eyes higher, along the back wall of the nave, you see a horizontal mural depicting personages from this historic time, including that of Mary Magdalene on bended knee offering Jesus her alabaster jar of spikenard with which she might anoint him. This reminds you of rituals of pagan goddesses or their priestesses who would anoint their consorts or kings. This continuity fills you with satisfaction that the Divine Union of Jesus and Mary Magdalene, a love story for lovers everywhere, was one chapter in a long book of pairings perpetuating harmony, unity, and wholeness between genders – and likewise within oneself. You get a sense of normalcy being restored as you imagine the lovers reunited.

Sitting in the darkness of Mary's holy place, time and distance dim. You try to imagine what it must have been like for women in centuries past. Perhaps you even see yourself garbed in the clothing of Mary's day, meeting covertly in the homes of other women, discussing how the old ways and the teaching of Jesus uplifted those the patriarchy might oppress, especially women. You remember having to school your sons and daughters in the old ways in secrecy. You recall those early struggles as monotheistic religion attempted to grab power from Goddess, and by association, women. You remember the frustration of universal truths being lost and normal relations between men and women being cast in a corrupting light as sexuality and intimacy between genders was now being deemed taboo. Divine Union, once the road to enlightenment, was now considered unclean. As a woman, you must now live your life behind the veil, lest you be branded a prostitute as was Mary Magdalene. Reflecting on these times past, you feel the frustration and fear of the overwhelming powers that be grip you, threatening you as a woman and giver of life.

Returning to the now, you shake off the shackles of the past and let your eyes revel in the images of the feminine faces of deity residing in every niche within the soothing darkness of this womb-like shrine. You look upon the powerful statue of Joan of Arc, the beloved Lady of Lourdes, and Mary, the mother of Jesus. You walk up to the central altar and again cast your eyes upward upon the powerful and majestic statue of Mary Magdalene, stars around her head, as she ascends to her celestial throne where she will sit beside her beloved. You see her opening her arms toward you, and with this simple gesture, your mind has been wiped clean of negativity. You can now more easily cast aside the programming that diminishes and denigrates. Here within this womb, new ideas freely gestate and are born. You imagine Mary's joy in washing the feet of her consort, him caressing her hair, and their warm embrace. The afterglow of their love for each over warms you.

You walk over to the bank of candles and light a wax torch in Mary's honor, and by doing so, symbolically shed light upon the darkness of ignorance and intolerance that divides and thwarts unity and wholeness. You feel compelled to reclaim that vibrant potency embodied within your own life force – your powerful femininity and sexuality. Being here has allowed you to give yourself permission to restore what might have once been lost or cast aside within your own life. You can bring yourself back to wholeness just as the Divine Couple is being restored to wholeness with today's new revelations.

Looking around her shrine, seeing all the aspects of the Sacred Feminine honored within these hallowed walls, you are inspired to be one in unity with the Divine Source, a microcosm of the macrocosm. Never again will you allow yourself to be oppressed, nor deny your true talents or nature. In visiting here you have been called to fulfill your purpose to be fruitful and blossom into fullness, never again hiding your light under a bushel because that might be more comfortable or expedient for another.

As you walk down the center aisle of La Madeleine toward the exit, these walls that once felt cavernous and abyss-like to you have since been transformed and in your mind are now a fortress that houses the deep repository of truths and mysteries of the Sacred Feminine. Turning back toward the altar for one last glimpse, you bow your head toward the images of Divine Feminine authority residing here. You thank them for reawakening you and make a silent promise to carry the light of the Sacred Feminine into the world.

When you are ready, gently open your eyes and return to the circle of our sacred space. Gently breathe and let your breath bring you back into awareness of this time and place. Wiggle your fingers and toes and speak your name out loud.

Chapter 31

Artemis – Independence and Autonomy

Find a comfortable place and ready yourself to make this sacred journey to your inner landscape. Breathe in and out. In and out. Try to follow the sound of my voice and see the images I suggest on the movie screen of your third eye. Breathe in and out. Slowly, breathe in and out. Let the cares and worries of the mundane world drop away. They are not important now. Breathe in and out. In and out. You are now ready to take your sacred pilgrimage.

You have traveled far, and you find yourself in Greece, or more specifically in Vravrona, the sacred locale of the nonconventional Goddess of light and darkness, life and death. There is an old woman sitting on the steps of the ruined temple, and she curls her finger in your direction, gesturing you come closer. She tells you it was here young girls called arktoi or "little she-bears" were schooled in the ways of the Goddess Artemis. The old woman laughs and says Artemis was no domestic Goddess! She asks you why you are here, and you say you are not quite sure. The old woman shakes her head knowingly and says, those called by Artemis are being challenged to dance to the drum beat of their own rhythms.

As you consider the words of the old woman, you realize you're already showing you are somewhat unconventional, venturing into Vravrona, a very industrialized area, rarely visited by tourists, though it is located just outside Athens. Yet, this quality is exactly the essence of the huntress Goddess, as followers of the Artemis archetype usually are more independent, self-sufficient and focused – even solitary, if necessary.

As you quietly walk among the standing stones, the last

remnants of the temple, you can almost hear the laughter of the young girls in training within the ancient complex as they dance in circles together, wearing their bear masks. You can imagine yourself dancing among the girls, wearing your own mask, reveling in the wild ecstasy of Nature herself. You surmise they learn not domestic chores, but instead, the art of hunting, the rules of the sacred landscape, herbology, and the other natural mysteries. This was not necessarily where one went to learn to be an obedient or subservient spouse. More likely, one would emerge from Vravrona expecting to participate in relationships of equality and partnership that included a healthy connection with all life, including the forest and the creatures living within it. The former arktoi would more than likely have grown into adults that embraced creativity and independence and embodied a wild streak that might have been somewhat hard to tame. These would be individuals who find it hard to depend on another.

If you are feeling called to this aspect of Artemis, you are being steered toward spending more time with Nature, an environment that nourishes you. Perhaps you have been relinquishing or suppressing too much of yourself for a relationship or job. Or maybe you have been holding back, afraid to set free that person lying dormant within you. Artemis is reminding you to embrace your personal liberty and find comfort living along the edges. Just take care to avoid being such an island unto yourself you become cut off from others or deny your emotional needs for intimacy. You may have to work at trust in relationships as your partnership skills may be rusty and suffer from your preference for isolation. Even followers of Artemis, like Nature herself, must strive for balance in all things.

As you turn back toward the old woman to ask her a question about the "little she-bears" who were trained here, she seems to have evaporated into thin air. Where could she have gone so suddenly? Then you realize your visit here was no accident and your presence has not gone unnoticed by the patroness of this sacred temple. You have been gifted with a rare and unique gift. You have been given a glimpse behind the veil at the face of Artemis in her mortal form. You know you must be true to your heart's calling.

As you reluctantly leave this sacred place holy to the Goddess so powerful the other gods would use her image as a sacred amulet, you promise to be true to your arktoi nature and trust in the sacred journey ahead that is your life.

Sit with those thoughts a minute, and when you are ready to return to us fully, open your eyes. Get up. Walk around. Have something to eat or drink.

Chapter 32

Ma'at – Feather of Truth

Please get comfortable and relax. Shake off any outside stress, concerns and fear. Breathe in and out. Breathe in and out. Allow yourself to see the suggestions from this meditation on the movie screen of your third eye. Breathe in to the count of five and out to the count of five. Do that several times. Allow yourself to feel grounded and connected. Center yourself.

Imagine yourself lying down in a cool, green meadow. Looking up, you see the bright sunshine, and you feel the warmth of its rays on your skin. You can hear the sound of running water from a cool and clear stream only feet before you. You feel you can relax. So you close your eyes as you soak in the essence and beauty of this place that you somehow know is very special, perhaps even sacred. Then there is a gentle touch on your arm, and you open your eyes to see your loved one is there with you. Your loved one beckons you to follow, so you get up and walk toward a grove of trees in the distance. You see a smile on your beloved's face, and you know instantly how much you are loved. You both continue walking, and soon you are immersed within the sacred grove.

You smell the freshness in the air. You take in the scent of the trees that remind you of days spent in Nature's embrace. Then suddenly before you both, you see a tumble of fallen pillars from a temple of days past. You follow your beloved as you both are being called to sit before a large, ancient altar stone. As you sit, you focus on your surroundings. You see the temple was once a beautiful place, and it still exudes an aura of potency. You hear the birds singing and see the rabbits frolicking among the long, green grass that has grown up among the stones. A delicious scent seems to fill the air, and you feel just a little bit intoxicated from the sweetness. It makes you want to close your eyes, relax and breathe in this once sacred place. You bask in the delicate sensations this place conjures within you.

You feel just a bit sleepy, with your eyes half shut; then all of a sudden you notice a mist collecting around one of the altar stones, the ancient inscription glowing. You look over at your beloved who you can tell sees it too. You are both mesmerized as you see the inscription becoming larger, clearer and more defined. You see the form of a woman holding a feather begin to take shape, shifting into a life-sized woman before you.

She has a kind face, and she smiles at you. Notice her straight black hair and the white feather she holds in her hands. As you are looking upon this wondrous, magical vision, you notice in the background that the temple is no longer a jumble of fallen stones. It is now the magnificent place it once was and still is for you and your beloved in this moment. You are standing on a marble floor. You feel the cold beneath your bare feet. You notice the sparkling gems in the crown upon this woman's head and the flowing robes that clothe her body.

She gestures to you to walk up the marble steps that will take you closer, and you willingly obey. Standing before her, you hear her begin to speak, "You are my child, my creation, whom I love with all my heart. Know that you may come to me anytime to unburden yourself, to avail yourself of my feathers of truth so you might set yourself free."

Your eyes meet, and you feel the sincerity in these words. You feel a warmth and a relief engulf your body. Ma'at continues, "You must be brave to carry my feather of truth. This is your time to transform and move into the next phase of life, to embrace new truths and let go of old ideas. This is that time for you to lay down the past. Allow, allow, allow yourself to become who you were meant to be. Throw off the shackles that bind your rebirth." The lady gestures for you to kneel before her, and she anoints you with the white feather she holds in her hand saying these healing words:

"Let what no longer serves you take flight. Lighten your mind and unburden yourself. Allow yourself to heal. Purify your mind from thoughts and deeds which hold no truth or life. You are being called to let go of those things that once shaped you, but they are no longer needed. Trust in me, my child. I am the Great Creatrix who blessed your mother's womb. You are perfect, and I love you unconditionally. Know that you may return to me here anytime you are troubled. I am within you and within all living things."

As Ma'at's voice trails off, you notice that the mist that formed her body begins to fade. You stand there in awe until the last molecules of her form have disappeared. Were you dreaming? Could this have actually happened? You turn around and look at the face of your beloved and touch the tears you see gently gathered. You know your beloved knows this Lady, and now you do too. You take the hand of your beloved, and you both silently walk down the marble steps. You can hardly believe what has just transpired.

As you look back over your shoulder, you see the ancient columns are once again in a jumble. The birds are flying overhead, and the rabbits are playing among the tall green grasses. You walk back through the sacred grove of trees to the spot alongside the stream where this journey began. You feel renewed. You feel loved. You feel protected. You know you are never alone.

When you are ready, allow yourself to open your eyes and return to our circle from where you started your journey. Allow yourself to continue to feel the emotions that came up for you in the meditation. They are a part of who you are. Rub your hands together. Wiggle your toes. Smile at the person next to you. Awaken from your journey, but retain the message for the days and weeks ahead.

Part IV

Resources and References

Suggested Resources

Please consider the following suggested resources as merely the tip of the iceberg and a jumping off point in your exploration and discovery of herstory, past, present and the potential future. As we recover the past and incorporate what wisdom we might glean to build a better tomorrow, we have so many dedicated voices to look to. I can hardly list them all here, and I apologize for anyone I may have omitted by accident. I ask your forgiveness.

Media

Voices of the Sacred Feminine Radio – **Blog Talk**
I would recommend listening to the new and archived shows collected over the past years on my internet radio show, *Voices of the Sacred Feminine*, found on Blog Talk Radio. I am honored to have interviewed so many wise and insightful women and men, and I whole-heartedly suggest you read their books, follow their work via their websites and watch their films. These are the people who will help reshape the world.

Grit TV
Free Speech TV
Democracy Now
Thom Hartman Talk Radio
Rachel Maddow Show
Sagewoman Magazine
Goddess Pages
Sacred History Magazine

Films/Documentaries

Avatar

Dangerous Beauty

Pope Joan

The East

Agora

Handmaiden's Tale

Iron Jawed Angels

The Magdalene Sisters

Femme: Women Healing the World

Dancing with Gaia

Divine Women Series (BBC)

Goddess Spirituality Trilogy: Goddess Remembered, Burning Times and Full Circle

Mea Maxima Culpa: Silence in the House of God

The End of Poverty

Inequality for All

Documentaries by Michael Moore

Pink Smoke Over the Vatican

Signs Out of Time

Red Tent Movie: Things We Don't Talk About

Blood Time, Moon Time, Dream Time

Groups/Organizations

The Goddess Temple of Orange County, Irvine, CA

The Goddess Studio, Escondido, CA

Ebenezer herchurch, San Francisco, CA

Isis Oasis Sanctuary, Geyserville, CA

Fellowship of Isis – U.S. & International

Circle Sanctuary, near Barneveld, Wisconsin

Sekhmet Temple of Goddess Spirituality, Cactus Springs, NV

Abbey of Avalon, Southern CA

Hands of Demeter, Southern CA
Riane Eisler's Center for Partnership Studies
Parliament of World Religions
Womanpriests
13 Indigenous Grandmothers
Lydia Ruyle/Goddess Icon Spirit Banners
Half the Sky Movement
Planned Parenthood
Emily's List
NARAL – ProChoice America
Feminist Majority Foundation
Code Pink

Teaching Resources

Obviously, as you read through the chapters of the book, take notes of the teachers and authors I mention who have inspired me. However, there are two outstanding curriculums available via the internet, which I believe should be required study for everyone; their bibliographies offer a vast wealth of resources:

Rise Up and Call Her Name (Elizabeth Fisher)
Cakes for the Queen of Heaven (Shirley Ranck)

Some Recommended Authors
(Fiction and Non-Fiction)

Barbara G. Walker
Selena Fox
Joan Norton
Jean Houston
Jean Shinoda Bolen
Merlin Stone
Mary Daly

Riane Eisler
Heide Gottner-Abendroth
Howard Zinn
Noam Chomsky
David Hillman
Cristina Biaggi
Marija Gimbutas
Starhawk
Nicholas Kristof
Joan Marler
Marguerite Rigoglioso
Elinor Gadon
Matthew Fox
Lucia Chiavola Birnbaum
Jann Aldredge-Clanton
Vajra Ma
Dharma Windham
Normandi Ellis
Isidora Forrest
Layne Redmond
Charlene Spretnak
Ava Park
Phyllis Chessler
Max Dashu
Harita Meenee
Jeannine Davis Kimball
Z Budapest
Jennifer Reif
Carol Christ
Patricia Monaghan
deTraci Regula
Linda Iles
Judy Foster
Sue Monk Kidd

Karen L. King
Alice Walker
Asphodel Long
Marion Zimmer Bradley
James Rietveld
Miriam Robbins Dexter
Margaret Starbird
Donna Henes

Songs and Music

We Sound a Call to Freedom/Mine Eyes Have Seen the Glory

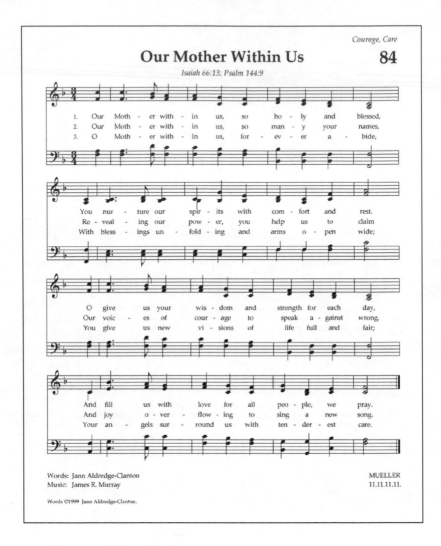

Courage, Care

Our Mother Within Us   84

Isaiah 66:13; Psalm 144:9

1. Our Moth - er with - in us, so ho - ly and blessed,
2. Our Moth - er with - in us, so man - y your names,
3. O Moth - er with - in us, for - ev - er a - bide,

You nur - ture our spir - its with com - fort and rest.
Re - veal - ing our pow - er, you help us to claim
With bless - ings un - fold - ing and arms o - pen wide;

O give us your wis - dom and strength for each day,
Our voic - es of cour - age to speak a - gainst wrong,
You give us new vi - sions of life full and fair;

And fill us with love for all peo - ple, we pray.
And joy o - ver - flow - ing to sing a new song.
Your an - gels sur - round us with ten - der - est care.

Words: Jann Aldredge-Clanton
Music: James R. Murray

MUELLER
11.11.11.11.

Words ©1999 Jann Aldredge-Clanton.

Our Mother Within Us/Away in a Manger

References

Part I

The Politics of Eco-Feminist Goddess Spirituality – A Thealogy for a Sustainable Future

1   Tate, Karen (2011, March 27) Original paper was presented at the annual meeting of the American Academy of Religion/WESCOR, Whittier College, Whittier, CA. Panel hosted by the Institute for Thealogy and Deasophy, titled Goddess Thealogy and Feminist Embodiments.

2   GRITtv Podcast: Nawal El Saadawi: What is Democracy, interviewed by Laura Flanders. Retrieved from http://www.freespeech.org/video/grittv-nawal-el-saadawi-what-democracy-0 and http://www.freespeech.org/category/tags/capitalism

3   Michaelson, P. (2011, February 23) The Primitive Conservative Psyche, BuzzFlash. Retrieved from http://blog.buzzflash.com/node/12395

4   Lakoff, G. (2011, February 19) What Conservatives Really Want, Truthout. Retrieved from http://www.truth-out.org/what-conservatives-really-want 67907

5   False Doctrine about the Holiness of Prosperity. Christian-Living-Site.com. Retrieved from http://www.christian-living-site.com/False-Doctrine-Prosperity.html

6   John Kenneth Galbraith. (n.d.). BrainyQuote.com. Retrieved from BrainyQuote.com Web site: http://www.brainyquote.com/quotes/quotes/j/johnkennet107301.html

7   "Liberals." Def. 2a., 5. Websters New Collegiate Dictionary 7th edition, 1974

8   Conservative vs. Liberal Beliefs. StudentNewsDaily.com.
     Retrieved from
     http://www.studentnewsdaily.com/conservative-vs-liberal-
     beliefs/

9   Ritual Human Sacrifice in the Bible. Fighting Against
     Immorality in Religion. Evil Bible.com.Retrieved from
     http://www.evilbible.com/Ritual_Human_Sacrifice.htm

10   Kennedy, Jr., Robert F. (2011, Feb 28) Regulators Reject
     proposal That Would Bring Fox-Style News to Canada.
     Retrieved from
     http://www.huffingtonpost.com/robert-f-kennedy-jr/fox-
     news-will-not-be-moving-into-canada-after-all_b_829473
     .html citing
     http://www.theglobeandmail.com/news/politics/ottawa-
     notebook/crtc-ditches-bid-to-allow-fake-news/article
     1921489/

11   Escobedo Shepherd, J. (2010, Nov 18) Republicans Vote
     Against Equal Pay For Women – Unanimously, AlterNet.
     Retrieved from
     http://www.alternet.org/newsandviews/article/339467/
     republicans_vote_against_equal_pay_for_women%E2%80%
     93unanimously/

12   UN Women: Facts & Figures on Women, Poverty and
     Economics citing UNICEF, 'Gender Equality" – The Big
     Picture', 2007. Retrieved from
     http://www.unifem.org/gender_issues/women_poverty
     _economics/facts_figures.php

13   The White House Project Report: Benchmarking Women's
     Leadership (2009, November). Retrieved from
     http://www.thewhitehouseproject.org/documents/
     Report.pdf

14   Poverty Among the Elderly Is a Women's Issue (2010,
     September) citing National Women's Law Center. Retrieved
     from

http://www.retirement-usa.org/blog/poverty-among-elderly
-women%E2%80%99s-issue

15 Harris-Perry, M (2011, March 3) The War on Women's
Futures. The Nation. Retrieved from
http://www.thenation.com/article/158981/war-womens-
futures

16 Tate, Karen (2010, August 20) Is Your Religion a Tier One or
Tier Two Religion? Only One Has True Freedom of Religion
Protections. The Examiner Los Angeles. Retrieved from
http://www.examiner.com/women-s-goddess-spirituality-
in-los-angeles/is-your-religion-a-tier-one-or-tier-two-
religion-only-one-has-true-freedom-of-religion-protections

17 Mahatma Gandhi. Quotationspage.com. Retrieved from
http://www.quotationspage.com/quotes/Mahatma_Gandhi

18 Braziel, D. (2010, September 15) 10 Poverty Statistics You
Can't Afford to Ignore.Change.org. Retrieved from
http://news.change.org/stories/10-poverty-statistics-you-
cant-afford-to-ignore

19 UPI -Washington (2011, Feb 3) 43 Million on Food Stamps.
Retrieved from
http://www.upi.com/Health_News/2011/02/03/USDA-43-
million-on-food-stamps/UPI-56301296757657/

20 Sherman, J. (2011, February 15) Politico. Federal job losses?
'So be it." Retrieved from
http://www.politico.com/news/stories/0211/49555.html

21 Homelessness (2011) Policyalmanac.org. Retrieved from
http://www.policyalmanac.org/social_welfare/homeless
.shtml

22 Karoli (2011, March 16) Gov. Rick Snyder Betrays Seniors for
Corporations, Crooks and Liars. Retrieved from
http://crooksandliars.com/karoli/gov-rick-snyder-betrays-
seniors-corporation

23 Jones, Sarah (2011, March 9) Rachel Maddow Exposes
Michigan Republicans Secret War on Democracy.

Politicususa.com. Retrieved from
http://www.politicususa.com/en/rachel-maddow-michigan

24 Celock, J. (2011, September 21) Ohio SB 5 Collective
Bargaining Law Follows Efforts in Wisconsin and New
Jersey. Huffington Post.Retrieved from
http://www.huffingtonpost.com/2011/09/20/ohio-sb5-refer-
endum-collective-bargaining_n_972321.html

25 Starr, B. (2011, January 3) We Are A Religions Nation – Or
Are We? Huffington Post. Retrieved from
http://www.huffingtonpost.com/bernard-starr/we-are-a-
religious-nation_b_802448.html

26 Lazonick, W. (2011, July 25) The Reason CEOs Make 350
Times More Money Than Their Workers – And Why That's
Terrible for the Economy. Alternet.Retrieved from
http://www.alternet.org/economy/151767/the_reason_
ceos_make_350_times_more_money_than_their_workers_—
_and_why_that%27s_terrible_for_the_economy/

27 Johnson, C. (2011, April 20) After Financial Crisis, Wheels of
Justice Turn Slowly. NPR. Retrieved from
http://www.npr.org/2011/04/20/135575032/after-financial-
crisis-wheels-of-justice-turn-slowly

28 Chan, V. (2010, January 25) Western Women Can Come to the
Rescue of the World. The Dalai Lama Center. Retrieved from
http://dalailamacenter.org/blog-post/western-women-can-
come-rescue-world

29 Rizzo, A. (2010, January 16) Vatican reviewers say 'Avatar' is
no movie masterpiece. Associated Press. Retrieved from
http://special.registerguard.com/csp/cms/sites/web/news
/cityregion/24351962-46/vatican-movie-nature-avatar-
cameron.csp

30 Villines, C.J. (2010, January 3) Conservative Christians vs.
Avatar. Retrieved from
http://www.religiondispatches.org/dispatches/culture/21
47/conservative_christians_v._avatar_

31   Why Women Should Vote. Snopes.com. Retrieved from
http://www.snopes.com/politics/ballot/womenvote.asp

Chapter 13 – Separating Truth from Myth

32   "More About Thanksgiving – An Introduction for Teachers"
Essay of Chuck Larsen, historian, teacher, author of several
books on American and Native American history
33   "The Plymouth Thanksgiving Story" by Chuck Larsen
34   "Invasion of America" by Francis Jennings
35   Manataka American Indian Council – http://www.manataka
.org

About the Author

For almost three decades, Karen's work has been fueled by her intense interest and passion for travel, comparative religions, ancient cultures, and the resurging interest in the rise of the Feminine Consciousness.

As an independent scholar, speaker, radio show host, published author, and social justice activist, Karen's body of work blends her experiences of women-centered multiculturalism evident in archaeology, anthropology and mythology with her unique academic and literary talents, coupled with her travel experience throughout the world. Her first book, *Sacred Places of Goddess: 108 Destinations,* has garnered prestigious endorsements, while her second book, *Walking an Ancient Path, Rebirthing Goddess on Planet Earth,* was a finalist in the National Best Books of 2008 Awards. Tate's work has been highlighted in the Los Angeles Times, Seattle Times and other major newspapers. She is interviewed regularly in print, on television and on national public radio, and she hosts her own radio show, *Voices of the Sacred Feminine,* considered a treasure trove of insight and wisdom for our time. Her work has segued into writing, producing and consulting on projects which bring the ideals and awareness of the Sacred Feminine into the mainstream world through television and film. She can be seen in the new documentary, **Femme: Women Healing the World**, produced by Wonderland Entertainment.

Contact Karen at:

ancientcultures@ca.rr.com